America's Gilded Age

Its Architecture and Decoration

Frederick Platt

South Brunswick and New York: A. S. Barnes and Company
London: Thomas Yoseloff Ltd

A. S. Barnes and Co., Inc.
Cranbury, New Jersey 08512

Thomas Yoseloff Ltd
108 New Bond Street
London W1Y OQX, England

Library of Congress Cataloging in Publication Data

Platt, Frederick, 1946–
    America's gilded age.

    Bibliography: p.
    Includes index.
    1. Eclecticism in architecture—United States. 2. Archi-
tecture, Modern—19th century—United States. 3. Architecture, Modern—20th century—United States. I. Title.
NA710.5.E25P42   720′.973   73–114
ISBN 0–498–01322–7

Contents

America's Gilded Age

Its Architecture and Decoration

1
Prologue

When the Civil War had ended, the United States found it was not what it had been, but was more. The industrial North had defeated the agrarian South, but the war only formalized the victory and may even have delayed the flowering of American industry. The long peace that followed—from 1865 to 1917, with little interruption—held no obstacle for either industry or industrious individuals. The United States, which had been a placid, uncertain, and relatively unimportant country before the Civil War, emerged during this period of over 50 years as an energized, rich, and powerful nation. Its architecture turned from the mainly folk and rural building of the antebellum era to the mighty and majestic art of the Gilded Age, thoroughly in the mainstream of world architecture and worthy of a place in it.

But it is characteristic of historians, whether of events or of architecture, that they do not consider an age interesting until it is far enough in the past that most of its evidence is lost. This attitude hinders the study of the Gilded Age and its architecture.

Historians of modern architecture, however, do not share this characteristic, since they have little regard for much of anything built before 1920. They have nothing but disdain for the main body of Gilded Age architecture, since it was the immediate predecessor of the modern and therefore the work against which modernism, with rebellion as a central tenet, would most likely seem to be in revolt. And this attitude hinders the study of Gilded Age architecture, and the age as a whole, since the era and its architecture are so tightly bound together.

Good nonarchitectural writing on the period has been done mainly about the poor, a group hardly brought to mind by the term "Gilded Age." The rich largely have been confined to gossipy books and awe-filled articles for the society-minded. Among intellectuals, aggravated poverty is currently all the rage —provided, of course, it is someone else's; even in the permissive present, wealth is always evil—provided, likewise, it is not one's own. This is still another hindrance to the study of the Gilded Age, and its architecture, since the rich built many of the period's most fascinating edifices.

That the period is not old enough will be solved by time, and time will also help those in the future see past the rejection of the era's architecture by the modernists and the hatred of the wealthy by intellectuals. But, for the present, what are the reasons behind these last two damaging objections? That which is true concerning other periods is especially true with the Gilded Age: to understand the era, not only must the facts be seen, but they must be seen without the prejudices of the present.

It ought not to be necessary to discuss prevalent opinions of Gilded Age millionaires when the period's architecture is being considered: art of any age should be judged for itself alone. Unfortunately, though, the reputations of the Gilded Age patrons have come to affect the very way the structures they built are seen, and an increase in regard for the era's wealthy raises regard for its architecture.

Most of the indictments against Gilded Age millionaires were much less adamant during that era itself than since. The Gilded Age ended at World War I, but a good part of its attitudes and architecture continued to the depression of 1929. The New Deal historians were searching for the causes of the money calamity, and since the most conspicu-

THOMAS ALVA EDISON
Calling himself a "bloated eastern manufacturer," Edison used the money of capitalists to improve the lives of people the world over.

ANDREW CARNEGIE
This famous tycoon retired from the steel business to devote himself to full-time philanthropy.

ous group connected with the previous era's finances were the millionaires, they were looked upon as malefactors whose sins had been visited on later generations. The millionaires were by no means free of all blame for the depression, but they hardly would have knowingly created a situation that would jeopardize their own fortunes and eventually make the existence of their own species impossible.

The most important book from the 1930s dealing with the Gilded Age is Matthew Josephson's *The Robber Barons*. It is a beautifully written classic, but a central summary of the New Deal view of the very rich. Due to the lack of concern of most historians with the Gilded Age, no equally good book has appeared to refute Josephson at length, and the impressive name Robber Barons has stuck fast to the era's millionaires. The term remembers the medieval thieves who would charge travelers exhorbitant tolls to cross mountain and river passes that the bandits controlled, and was first applied to the Gilded Age millionaires by the Populists in the 1880s.

The robbers of the Middle Ages were as much barons as the barons of the Gilded Age were robbers. P. A. B. Widener, the traction magnate, was fond of saying he got ahead in business because he was honest. His namesake, writing in 1940 about his grandfather, said he doubted this would be true by later standards, but that is was by the standards of his grandfather's era. Gould and Fisk were crooks, no question of it, but the majority of the millionaires were honest—even in their own eyes.

They may have been honest—at least to the point of not being arrested—but were they ethical? Their modern detractors harangue that the millionaires had become rich by forcing millions of people to live on subsistence wages and to give up health and life working in inhuman factories and mines. Even if this were true, judgment is again being made by the standards of the present, as cruel as this apology might sound. It seemed natural at the time for an employer to work his help as long and hard as he was able, and to give to the employee in return as little as possible. The average worker did not feel himself a victim of his boss. Many of the millionaires had worked their way up from circumstances similar to those of their employees, yet these Horatio Alger characters saw no reason for reform.

A person's bad aspects are usually much more interesting to other people than his good ones, so it is little wonder the Gilded Age millionaires, who had a chance to do both good and evil on a gigantic scale, have been remembered more for their wrongdoing than for their beneficence. Many contributions the rich made during this period continue as gifts to the people of today. Many of their direct donations to the public can be seen in these pages: the wealthy gave museums, libraries, music halls, hospitals, churches, and entire universities. A great deal of the European and Oriental art now in the United States was brought here originally during the Gilded Age for the collections of millionaires, who later often bequeathed their treasures to the public; the heart of the National Gallery collection is still the gifts of Mellon, Kress, and Widener, three patrons of one of the gallery's founding forces, Lord Duveen.

Harder to comprehend, but more important, is the improvement the millionaires made in the daily lives of the people, of not only the United States but the world. American history is economic history: the foremost movers in the nation's development were its capitalists. In their efforts to make money and increase their personal empires, they brought about growth in technology and invention that raised the standards of living throughout the world, and to the highest on earth in the United States.

Gilded Age architecture is the inheritance that the present most clearly connects with the millionaires of that past era. The Gilded Age was a period of grand architecture, and grand architecture implies grand money; many of the most wonderful buildings of the times were erected by the millionaires for themselves, their corporations, or the public. The many remaining commercial and public structures from the Gilded Age are admired by their present-day users, who have been taught not to expect such grandeur and humanity from modern architecture. Residences of that past era still serve their original purpose or now are homes to businesses, schools, museums, or other institutions. A number are maintained as museums of themselves, since a spectacular Gilded Age mansion is as worthy of display in its own right as any other work of art. Hard as it may be to admit, many treasures from the Gilded Age—and from most of the world's great ages of art—would never have been created but for the rich.

Current opinion on Gilded Age architecture is harmed far more by its condemnation by modern architects and their apologists than by the sad reputation of the era's millionaires. Weight is given the criticism by the modernists because, for one thing, buildings in the newer style have become so ubiquitous as to give the appearance of an artistic victory by the modern over the traditional styles. For another, the theories that govern modern architecture grew from the same beliefs that now greatly influence almost every aspect of contemporary thought. These beliefs have become so basic they are often unquestioned, and using them it would be impossible to imagine an architecture different from the modern.

Of course, the modernists do not despise every architect that flourished during the Gilded Age. When the modern style began to emerge full-force in the 1920s, its followers liked to pretend it had emerged full-grown from the blue, having no history because it turned its back on the history of styles. But in fact all art movements have roots, and modern architecture turned out to have very deep ones, as the modernists later gladly acknowledged, when the modern, now become respectable, set out to discover its family tree. The modernists quite correctly found in their lineage such famous Gilded Age architects as Frank Furness, Henry Hobson Richardson, and Louis Sullivan. It should not be forgotten that Frank Lloyd Wright, master of the modern, produced his early buildings during the Gilded Age.

The kindest present-day modernists allow some merit to some Gilded Age styles—for their day, of course: only the most modern of modern design can be used for today's construction. Acceptance of a building from that earlier era is based upon the design's adherence, real or imagined, to modern tenets. For example, praise is often given a Gilded Age style in amounts proportionate to its obscurity, since obscurity suggests originality, a passion (but not too often a practice) of modern architects. The most prevalent, but still barely allowable, style used during the Gilded Age is the Gothic. But almost never will the modernists applaud the Gilded Age's central style, and that in which most of the era's great structures were built, the classical, the style derived from Greece, Rome, and the Renaissance.

In order to view without bias the architecture of the Gilded Age (and of other ages, including the modern), it is necessary to tear down some of the walls of protective theory the modernists have built up around their favorite style.

Theory is the backbone of modern architecture. The modernists see with their minds instead of their eyes. To judge a building, they decide how closely it conforms with modern theories; if the building fits the theories, it wins approval—no matter how ugly it might appear to the common beholder. These theories are expanded by modernists in an endless flow of words; to become known as a good modern architect, it is helpful to have ability at writing. The modernists derive their theories not from architectural practice, but from sundry unrelated subjects, such as psychology, sociology, and so on, and build up a world view, then create an architecture worthy of a place in their philosophy. The emphasis on acquiring an overall outlook, rather than on learning architectural craftsmanship, leads the modernists to regard architecture more as a religion than as an art, which accounts for their shocked view of heretical disbelievers.

It is one of the absurdities of the modern that its true followers must walk such a straight-and-narrow path, when one of its central tenets is originality.

Architects through the ages have rarely exhibited originality as one of their most prominent traits, and modern architects, with originality as an objective, have usually felt safer all being original in the same way. The rejection by the modernists of all but strict modern style for buildings today being erected has left the modern architect with only his strict modern predecessors to copy. This explains why most modern structures look so much alike. Ironically, modernism's arch enemy, the classical, provides through its gigantic variety of elements the chance both to copy and to be original.

The tendency of all architecture to copy would normally allow modern architecture to fulfill easily another modernist requirement: a building should be an expression of the time and region for which it is designed. The similarities of structures from any one age and area are usually enough apparent to permit ready identification of the building's origins. The hardest cases of guessing are created by the modern, or International Style, as it is often called by the same modernists that espouse the theory of reflecting time and place. That theory is bound up with the modernists' hatred of history (except for the movement's own past). But what is here and now? When did the classical style, which has been useful to man for over 2,500 years, suddenly lose its meaning? At what political boundary does the importance of the Gothic end? Hardly any building, even a modern one, can help but denote the time and place of its design. The modern architect would seem unnecessarily concerned over a requirement he is least equipped to meet.

Another needless worry of the modern architect is the value he places on being progressive. Art, man's creation, cannot progress without progress in the basic composition of men, which has been such a slow process that progress could not have been made in the period of time from the Parthenon to the buildings of Le Corbusier. (And who could detect progress by using these two benchmarks?) The modernists confuse progress with procession, thinking that because art has history, the changing of art epochs represent improvement.

Further fallacies are labeled "rationalism" and "functionalism" and "naturalism," three recurring words in the theory of modern architecture. The first two as used architecturally are basically synonyms, the second being the more widely used today; the third is closely related.

Rationalism-functionalism preaches that a building's design ought to be derived from nothing more than its use. This precludes almost any artistic embellishment or decoration. The result is the endless number of bland, unadorned buildings seen everywhere. "Man can live without ornament," says the modernist. The classicist replies, "Yes, but not very well."

Functionalism was brought on by man's lack of confidence in man. When man has a low opinion of himself, he cannot see why he should be surrounded by beauty. The first appearance in America of functionalism came about 1820, when the Romantic Era arrived from Europe on the shores of the struggling young country. The romantics quieted their fears by creating theoretical civilizations, not coming face to face with the real one. Their architectural dreams were not of grander buildings and ornaments, as happy minds might desire, but for plainer ones. When the Gilded Age restored greater optimism to the nation, functionalism was overwhelmed by classicism and other affirmative styles. But when World War I brought an end to the Gilded Age and its optimism, and when the modern world steeped in self-doubt emerged, functionalism almost entirely captured architecture.

Naturalism stresses the close ties between nature and modern architecture. Love for nature can only surpass its companions, awe and respect, when man has sufficient control over his surroundings to be able for the most part to shut out nature at will. The early European settlers in America, living in untouched nature, felt themselves not so much a part of nature as apart from it; they had to struggle for their lives against snow, disease, and bear. By the Romantic Era, beginning around 1820, nature in America, at least in the East, was so well tamed that it could be regarded as an amiable playmate. Architecture could now become the child of nature, which it largely did, and has mainly remained, except for the central body of Gilded Age architecture. The taming of nature, however, only allowed man to become its admirer; it was the pessimism of the Romantic and modern eras that set man to turn to nature rather than man as his guide.

Among the results of naturalism are those famous houses supposed to "blend in" with their surroundings. A more affirmative view might be that a house of noble design—for instance, in the classical style— would ennoble the surroundings, beautifying nature

rather than hiding behind it. In city buildings, where rusticity is downright impossible, the modernists talk of retaining "the integrity of materials," displaying building materials for their own merit, never realizing that carved marble possesses not only the beauty of the marble, but also the beauty of the carving. When the modernist allows ornament, it is often provided by trees and other greenery, rather than statues of the menacing figure of man. Should a commemorative bust of the human after whom a public building is named be absolutely unavoidable, the modern sculptor will distort the figure, glorifying the subject's individual character, rather than his species.

If, for a moment, architecture is granted the importance the modernists give it, it will be seen that modern architecture in its pessimism renders its beholders pessimistic. Le Corbusier thought revolution in architecture forestalled revolution in society. But the architecture he believed in has not brought stability; it has engendered revolution, rather than averting it.

The Romantic Era introduced rational theory into American architecture. The rules were nowhere near as harshly applied as they are in modern design; the human thirst for architectural decoration and variety had not yet been sufficiently suppressed. The resulting architecture was of that collection of styles often called American Victorian. While the theories behind these styles may be questionable, the buildings are picturesque and really very friendly.

American Victorian architecture was heavily influenced by the Gothic style, since that gift of the Middle Ages was thought to take its design from its function. Architects such as Andrew Downing and Calvert Vaux used the American interpretation of the Gothic to create endearing rural structures for what was still a rural America.

The Gilded Age changed the complexion of American civilization, and of the nation's architecture. The new age saw the rise of the cities, in which American Victorian was, for the monumental new buildings, practically unworkable. The emerging personal empires of the new tycoons could not express wealth, power, and grandeur through the rural building of the previous era. The nation as a whole now turned, as it had during colonial and federal days, to the style its government almost alone had kept using in construction during the Romantic Era: that style was the classical.

Of course, the change did not come overnight. The Gilded Age for its first fifteen years (1865-1880), during which the age was awakening to its own potential but not yet at the full force of its kinetic energy, retained American Victorian as its reigning styles. After that, American architecture entered a transitional period, typified by the shingle style of the countryside during the 1880s. While much has been made of this style's connections with modern architecture, connections more direct are between the shingle style and the then moribund architecture of the Romantic Era, the period whose theories were revived in the making of modernism. The lively elements of the shingle style seem to be actually preclassical. McKim, Mead and White, leading workers in the shingle style, later became leading classicists, not by turning their backs on the shingle style, but

partly by developing it. That firm's Newport Casino (shown later in this volume), the best of all shingle style buildings, certainly contains the essence of classicism in its order and symmetry. Many of the transition's best nonclassical structures hint at the coming classicism. Richardson, with his tendency toward monumentality, might well have been designing in the classical style, had he lived ten years longer.

The architecture of the transition is amply illustrated throughout this book. The American Victorian that had been previously prevalent, as well as the arrival in force of classicism, can be seen by inspecting two Gilded Age world's fairs.

The Centennial Exposition was held in 1876 at Fairmount Park in the nation's birthplace, Philadelphia. The fair mirrored the young Gilded Age. The most impressive sight for most visitors was the gigantic Corliss steam engine. Here was a symbol of the age: industrial, energetic, technological, mighty. There were other reflections, too, such as

Philadelphia, Pennsylvania　　　　　*Henry Joseph Schwarzman, Architect*
CENTENNIAL EXPOSITION—JUDGES' HALL

]14[

Philadelphia, Pennsylvania   *Henry Joseph Schwarzman, Architect*
CENTENNIAL EXPOSITION—BUILDING OF THE PENNSYLVANIA STATE COMMISSIONERS

Philadelphia, Pennsylvania   *Henry Joseph Schwarzman, Architect*
CENTENNIAL EXPOSITION—MEMORIAL HALL

]15[

Alexander Graham Bell demonstrating his new invention, the telephone.

A selection of centennial buildings by the fair's chief architect, Henry Joseph Schwarzman, is shown here. Varied traditions inspired the buildings illustrated, but all except one are in a romantic, picturesque vein. This is perfectly acceptable, considering the park setting, the ephemeralness of the event, and the impermanence of the structures. None of the romantic structures, however, would have been suitable for the cities of twenty years later. One building shown, Memorial Hall, was constructed to be permanent. The edifice was intended to be the public art museum for Philadelphia after the close of the fair, and so it was until it was superseded in the 1920s by a larger, new building. Currently Memorial Hall houses public sports facilities. For this permanent building, Schwarzman chose the classical style: it was, after all, the favorite style of government, for whose use following the exposition it was meant. At the time of this fair, American architecture, as reflected in the exposition buildings, was still centered around romanticism, but contained examples of the classicism soon to sweep the nation.

If during the 1890s there was any question left what style would dominate the Gilded Age, it was

Chicago, Illinois

WORLD'S COLUMBIAN EXPOSITION—COURT OF HONOR
The building to the left is Agricultural Hall by Charles Follen McKim, that to the right the Manufactures and Liberal Arts Building by George B. Post, and that at the center the Administration Building by Richard Morris Hunt. Daniel Chester French was the sculptor of the statue of *The Republic* in the front of the picture. (Courtesy Chicago Historical Society)

answered with finality by the World's Columbian Exposition, held at Chicago in 1893. How can the event be praised enough? It was simply the best single monument to the United States and its art to that time or since. More than any other element, it was the architecture that set the tone of the fair; the buildings, almost to a one, were classical. The architects of the fair were from among the finest of the Gilded Age. Daniel H. Burnham was the chief architect, and he invited such as Richard Morris Hunt, Charles Follen McKim, Stanford White, and George B. Post; their names echo through this book. The most spectacular feature of the fair's architecture was the Court of Honor; mirrored in its reflecting pool was the triumph of classicism and of a nation.

Interior decoration during the Gilded Age underwent the same changes of style as did architecture. In the Romantic Era, the furnishings had been of the same American Victorian style as the buildings that housed them, and they so remained well into the new age. The picturesque notion of interior decoration was codified in Charles Locke Eastlake's *Hints on Household Taste in Furniture, Upholstery and Other Details,* which was first published in London in 1868 and in America four years later, and widely read and obeyed. The book lauded especially the Gothic for its supposed functionalism. While the Gilded Age approved of many styles, it discovered it needed the classical as its central style, and the change to the predominance of the classical began around 1880, in interior decoration as in architecture.

It is difficult to realize what was implied in the Gilded Age by the words "interior decoration." A modern architect generally decides how the rooms of one of his structures is to be finished, if not furnished; that is, he will determine how the ceilings, walls, and floors will appear, and what built-in lighting fixtures and so on will be used. In cases of commercial or public buildings, or expensive houses, he often will even design the furniture or see to its arrangement. While Gilded Age architects were certainly equipped to do this—many were hired to do interior decorating for older homes—the architects of that time often provided only the exterior of a building; both finishing and furnishing of the interior were left to an interior decoration firm, such as J. Allard et Fils, Alavoine et Cie., or Carlhian of London. These firms would finish the visible walls, ceilings, and floors for many or all a building's rooms, provide interior staircases and the like, and gather antique furniture or collect or manufacture new. Notice is seldom paid to these firms whose contributions to art are greatly admired.

Gilded Age interior decoration is not the clutter and oppressiveness many people picture it. True, there were acres of oak paneling, but it was enlivened with gold leaf, paint, and carving. True, there were ballrooms containing armor displays on wooden, full-size horses and knights, but these ballrooms were appropriately of medieval design, and big enough to handle such figures. True, there were some absolutely dreadful rooms to be seen, but this is true for all eras. Then there were the white-and-gold rooms, the solariums, the potted palms, the Japanese vases, the paintings by Sargent. The optimistic Gilded Age would not have stood for interior decoration that did not share the era's outlook.

The first interior decorator as known today was Elsie de Wolfe. Originally from Halifax, she became a daring New York socialite. She tried the theater in the 1890s, but, especially after losing her own money in a show in which she appeared, decided her field was interior decoration. From her little house, which still stands on Irving Place, she went forth to decorate the homes of many wealthy people. Her contemporaneity as an interior decorator is attested to by an acquaintance's comment that Miss de Wolfe could not spend more than 15 minutes in a room without wanting to rearrange the furniture. Her taste was really excellent; her rooms were the height of elegance. But she was not an interior decorator in the full sense of Gilded Age decorating firms; she was a rearranger.

Today, her spiritual descendants—although hardly her equals—are the little ladies sent out from shoppes to talk of "color accents" and "fun pieces," and are the customers who believe in those little ladies and have a passion for leafing through current decorating magazines, and are the people who, in Newport's Marble House, standing in the Gold Room, with its copious gilt, its chandeliers with angels at trumpets, and its Allard mantelpiece of bronze figures, will say, "It's too busy."

ELSIE DE WOLFE
In that section of her Irving Place, New York City home she called her "cozy corner."

In the remaining chapters, all but the last, there is a selection of Gilded Age buildings erected from 1880 to 1915. Structures from the first fifteen years of the age are very rarely included since they are usually demonstrations more of the architecture of the Romantic Era than that of the Gilded Age; buildings after 1915 that continue Gilded Age traditions are treated by themselves in the last chapter, since technically those structures were built after the Gilded Age. Classification of a building into a chapter is by its original use, and, within the chapter, in most cases by its date, oldest to newest.

The selection is not mathematically representative of the entire body of buildings of the Gilded Age. The structures included were usually commissioned by wealthy individuals or organizations; the Gilded Age is remembered for its grand buildings, and, besides, these are simply more interesting. While some buildings less than the best—*de gustibus non est disputandum*—are allowed here, most of the build-

ings are the cream of the period; one bad building speaks volumes. A great architect may have a greater number of buildings shown here than does his lesser contemporary; the great architects generally received the grandest commissions and designed the best buildings. A wide variety of styles is shown herein; if classical predominates these pages, that is because it did the same to the age.

This book may prove useful to a number of individuals. The architectural traditionalist might find it convinces people of the truth of his tenets (but the modernist might discover it confirms that of his own); with all the words flying in architecture, it might just help to show some buildings. The person interested in the Gilded Age as a whole might consider the book helpful; one cannot understand the Gilded Age without understanding its architecture. Then there is the person who plain likes to look at pictures of beautiful things.

2
Houses in the City

*T*he Gilded Age had a very different view of the city than has the present, even though that past era, through its railroads and motorcars, began today's exodus of many of the middle and upper classes from the city. During the Gilded Age, the city was still the absolute hub of human activity, and the glorification of the city was considered a duty of the architect.

Classicism, early in the Gilded Age, proved again to be the ideal style for city grandeur, and with classicism came the City Beautiful movement, which consisted of urban planning on classical lines. According to the movement, not only did separate buildings have to be beautiful, but so did their situation to one another, as did their landscaping, including fountains and fireplugs. Out of the City Beautiful movement came such marvels as the 1901 McMillan Commission plan for the nation's capital; Burnham and Bennett's Chicago Plan of 1907; Park Avenue and the closing of that axis by two 1913 buildings that Whitney Warren designed; and, in Philadelphia, the Benjamin Franklin Parkway, begun in 1917 from the plans of Jacques Greber.

Even more important than the wealth of classical architecture and planning to the livability of the Gilded Age city was the attitude of the people toward the city. Poverty was no less rampant, nor was dirt, nor crime. But the optimism of the Gilded Age allowed people to see the city as beautiful; they believed in man, and so in man's achievement, the city. Just as the modernist hates classical art, which is the most human design, and just as he hates beauty, which is the most human aesthetic concept, so he hates the city, which is the habitat of humanity. He despises man, and seeks the place where man is not; he must always be disappointed, for he himself is man, and so can never enter such a place.

Residence of James G. Blaine
Washington, District of Columbia

John Fraser, *Architect*

This house can be found in almost any American city. The building is what most people envision when they think of an American Victorian house. This particular house is an especially fine American Victorian mansion; its architect was John Fraser, who also designed such Victorian structures as the 1865 Union League Club of Philadelphia. The Washington house was built in 1881, and was the residence of James G. Blaine, the politician and three-time unsuccessful candidate for president.

Despite the apparent complexity that first greets the eye, a longer inspection will reveal the house to be relatively undecorated, relying more on the arrangement of its components than on their individual beauty. In this way is American Victorian architecture closely related to modern, and similar theory inspired both.

But these Victorian houses could hardly be considered modern, and many of those old residences are good, big, solid buildings, worthy of preservation. Those too big for most present-day families can assume such uses as restaurants or offices—the Blaine mansion is now a collection of law offices—and smaller versions make for comfortable family living.

Washington, District of Columbia　　　　　*John Fraser, Architect*
RESIDENCE OF JAMES G. BLAINE

Residence of Ross Winans

Baltimore, Maryland

McKim, Mead and White, *Architects*

The shingle style, which will be seen later in this book to have been so popular for country and resort buildings, was, because of its basic rusticity, unsuitable for city construction. It did, however, lend some of its elements to a number of city structures, which successfully incorporated them. One of these buildings is the 1882 Baltimore residence that Mc-Kim, Mead and White designed for Ross Winans, the locomotive designer.

A stone level supports two brick stories which, in turn, carry a gable roof. The free shape of the house is reminiscent of the coating of shingles with which the shingle style covers its freely placed collection of rooms. Two towers are prominent, one on the street side and one at the rear of the house. These towers are so modest they might really be considered elaborate bays—the tower in the rear, for example, contains the ballroom bay. They resemble the bays that are common features of the shingle style. Plaques of original designs are found on the exterior of walls, towers, and dormers; similar plaques are to be seen on Ochre Point, a shingle style Newport cottage by the same architects. (It is illustrated elsewhere herein.)

The shingle style did make several attempts to enter full form into the city, but such buildings were never successful. However, adaptations of the shingle style, like the still-standing Winans house, did win acceptance.

Baltimore, Maryland   *McKim, Mead and White, Architects*
RESIDENCE OF ROSS WINANS

Residence of William Kissam Vanderbilt

New York, New York

Richard Morris Hunt, *Architect*

No house played a more significant part in turning the nation's architecture away from the Victorian and toward the traditional than did the New York City residence of William Kissam Vanderbilt. The architect for the building was Richard Morris Hunt. A student at the École des Beaux Arts in Paris from 1846 to 1851, he designed an addition to the Louvre before returning home in 1855. Here he became a leading architect in the romantic styles then popular. When he received the Vanderbilt commission in 1879, however, he realized the old styles would not be sufficient for the new building, which was intended by Vanderbilt's wife, the tyrannical Alva, to mark the Vanderbilts' entry into New York society.

And so Hunt brought a new grandeur to American architecture; the Vanderbilt house was a limestone building in actual French Renaissance style. There had been Renaissance houses built during the Gilded Age before the Vanderbilt residence, but never anything so elaborate, detailed, or beautiful.

Mrs. Vanderbilt got her wish; the Vanderbilt family was thoroughly accepted in society, even by Mrs. Astor, beginning with the 26 March 1883 housewarming ball, remembered as one of the greatest parties of the Gilded Age. A new age of architecture had also arrived, and the other architects took notice. The rising Charles Follen McKim frequently took a walk in the evening to see the house; he said he slept better for having seen it.

New York, New York   *Richard Morris Hunt, Architect*

RESIDENCE OF WILLIAM KISSAM VANDERBILT

Residence of Cornelius Vanderbilt
New York, New York
George B. Post, *Architect*

The transition from Victorian to traditional was not always made so readily as with the W. K. Vanderbilt mansion. A number of houses built during the 1880s and 1890s and even thereafter were in a combination of the styles. Certainly this was the case with the mansion of Cornelius Vanderbilt, brother of W. K., grandson of the Commodore, and eventual builder of The Breakers in Newport, a structure shown later in these pages.

George B. Post, a disciple of Richard Morris Hunt, was the architect for the New York edifice. Begun in 1883, the original mansion occupied the northwest corner of Fifth Avenue and Fifty-seventh Street, but was soon extended up the Avenue to cover the entire block front to Fifty-eighth Street, where a grand entrance, with a high fence, park, and porte-cochère overlooked the Grand Army of the Republic Plaza. (The house was demolished in 1924.) Built of red brick trimmed in white marble, the mansion was fashioned after Fontainebleau, although elements of other styles, particularly Victorian, were present.

From buildings such as this one came the architectural term, "eclectic," which means the architect combined in one structure some touches of various older styles. Today, often the word is mistakenly applied to Gilded Age architecture as a whole. It will be seen, however, that almost every Gilded Age building is in its particular single style. Even eclectic buildings can be said to be of a consistent style, since they are each in their own style that was developed out of preceding styles. As for the artistic merit of an eclectic house, once the observer accustomed to modern blandness recovers from the initial look of complexity of those older structures, he will find that the elements generally blend very well, that there is a certain order to their arrangement, and the individual details are usually very beautiful.

New York, New York   *George B. Post, Architect*
RESIDENCE OF CORNELIUS VANDERBILT

RESIDENCE OF CORNELIUS: VANDERBILT—ENTRANCE HALL

Residence of Louis Comfort Tiffany

New York, New York

McKim, Mead and White, *Architects*

The 1884 mansion that Stanford White, of McKim, Mead and White, designed for Louis Comfort Tiffany was a last peak in the development of the romantic construction that had possessed American architecture for several decades; to this summation was added the size and grandeur that was to typify the incoming age of building. A classical house would have been almost inappropriate in this case, since its owner, the glassware designer, was a leading champion of romantic art.

The style of the edifice is part Queen Anne, which was the basis of the shingle style architecture of the countryside, and part medieval. Upon a base of rock-face masonry sit upper stories with a recessed center section that divides the facade in three, all the divisions terminating in gables protruding from the gigantic gable roof. The overall shape of the mansion is really very basic: four walls and a gable roof, but with a turret at the outside corner of the building. Overall, the structure might be seen as a spectacular romantic version of an everyday object, rather like the products of its patron.

New York, New York   *McKim, Mead and White, Architects*
RESIDENCE OF LOUIS COMFORT TIFFANY

Residences of Louis Henry Villard and Others

New York, New York

McKim, Mead and White, *Architects*

The residence of Henry Villard, president of the Northern Pacific Railroad as well as a backer of Thomas Edison, was one of five conjoined townhouses beneath a single exterior. Stanford White had done most of the planning for the 1885 house, but the exterior was left to Joseph Morrill Wells, a draftsman in the firm of McKim, Mead and White. Wells based his design upon the Cancelleria in Rome.

The Villard edifice is built around three sides of a courtyard. The high basement with square windows and the first floor with arched ones have rusticated walls, while the second, third, and top floors. with rectangular, arched, and square windows, respectively, have not. The material was to have been light stone, probably limestone, but unfortunately Villard requested brownstone, that stone of Victorian New York townhouses.

The building is now occupied mainly by the Roman Catholic Archdiocese of New York. This organization will soon move, and the handsome building will probably be demolished.

New York, New York   *McKim, Mead and White, Architects*

RESIDENCES OF HENRY VILLARD AND OTHERS

Residence of P. A. B. Widener

Philadelphia, Pennsylvania

Willis G. Hale, *Architect*

Although American Victorian houses generally had some little decoration, they were not often lavishly decorated, and this plainness seemed to come from their very nature. The P. A. B. Widener mansion, built in Philadelphia in 1886 with Willis G. Hale as architect, was essentially an American Victorian structure, but it was decorated profusely. The problem was that American Victorian architecture simply could not accommodate such display, and the result was a rather fearsome hodgepodge, no part of which looks at ease with any other part. Yet the Gilded Age was intent upon elaborate decoration, and it was this desire that drove the era toward the classical, the style that can best handle decoration, and in fact revels in it.

Widener, his growing family, and his growing art collection outgrew the house after fourteen years, and escaped to a magnificent Gilded Age estate in Elkins Park, Pennsylvania (the house illustrated in the next chapter). The town mansion was then given to the Free Library of Philadelphia, that city's municipal library. Today the building is occupied by an organization of ministers. The house may be an architectural curiosity, but it ought to be preserved for exactly that reason, as well as its connection with the famous financier, P. A. B. Widener.

Philadelphia, Pennsylvania   *Willis G. Hale, Architect*
RESIDENCE OF P. A. B. WIDENER

Residence of Alexander Van Rensselaer

Philadelphia, Pennsylvania

Peabody and Stearns, *Architects*

As a style for private homes, the classical found wide acceptance during the Gilded Age first in city houses. The classical mansions of Peabody and Stearns were enjoying a great vogue by 1890 in the architects' home city of Boston. Surprisingly, one of their best Boston classical houses was erected that year at Philadelphia overlooking Rittenhouse Square, a park very fashionable then among the aristocracy.

The original owner of the house was Alexander van Rensselaer, commodore of the Corinthian Yacht Club.

The main facade consists of a pair of bays the height of the house, which surround a center section that presents an entrance portico. A servants' wing to the north of the building is set behind a service court.

The mansion was for many years occupied by the Penn Athletic Club, which recently vacated it. It is now up for rent from its owners, the Presbyterian Ministers Fund.

Philadelphia, Pennsylvania　　　　　　*Peabody and Stearns, Architects*
RESIDENCE OF ALEXANDER VAN RENSSELAER

Residence of Bryan Lathrop

Chicago, Illinois

McKim, Mead and White, *Architects*

Georgian was a popular style for Gilded Age American mansions not only for its handsome appearance but also because of its English connotations to an Anglophilic aristocracy. Built at Chicago in 1892, the Bryan Lathrop house, now the Fortnightly Club, is a good example of American achievement in the style. McKim, Mead and White designed the house, but almost all architectural firms of the period were called upon to produce Georgian residences.

The facade of the Lathrop house is arranged in a flat center section between a pair of large bays. A flight of stairs from the pavement narrows as it approaches the balustraded landing set in front of the high basement. The first story is the most elaborate of the building's three floors, all in brick. Every facade window is rectangular, but the windows and rectangular door of the first story are placed in arches, the three arches of the center section being filled above the windows with delicate decoration. The door is within the left of the center section's arches, this positioning being one of the few exceptions to the symmetry of the structure. The top of the first story presents a wide stringcourse, above which the two upper stories have narrow bands at the level of the window sills. The three windows on the second floor of the center section, and the center window of the third floor, reach down below these levels to open onto the balconies, now removed.

Chicago, Illinois *McKim, Mead and White, Architects*

RESIDENCE OF BRYAN LATHROP

(Courtesy Chicago Historical Society, Photo by Carol Rice)

Residence of Mrs. William B. Astor

New York, New York

Richard Morris Hunt, *Architect*

Caroline Schermerhorn Astor, *the* Mrs. Astor, had come to rule New York society while still living in her brownstone house at 350 Fifth Avenue. It was to allow for the size of her ballroom there that Ward McAllister first chose "The 400." A family feud saw her nephew-in-law, William Waldorf Astor, build next door the start of a very famous hotel (the rest of this story being in the chapter on hotels), and fearing for her privacy, Mrs. Astor was forced to move. She may even have been relieved to have an excuse for moving, since most of the rest of society was already further uptown.

Richard Morris Hunt was commissioned to design Mrs. Astor's new house at Fifth Avenue and Sixty-fifth Street. An elaborate French chateau, the structure opened in 1895 to as great acclaim as had greeted Alva Vanderbilt's chateau a dozen years earlier. The Astor house was actually a double mansion: the recently-widowed Mrs. Astor lived in half of it and her son, John Jacob, and his wife, Ava, lived in the other half. For special occasions, the dividing doors could be parted. The complete ballroom held 1,200 people.

Mrs. Astor died in 1908 and her son aboard the *Titanic* in 1912. His son, Vincent Astor, occupied the house to 1925, when, after a final ball, it was sold to Benjamin Winter, who built the current Temple Emanu-El on the site.

In large part, the Astors got the money to build grand houses through real estate holdings: the family was known as the "landlords of New York." Of the tenements associated with the waves of immigrants that arrived in New York City during the Gilded Age, many buildings belonged to the Astors. Because of the poverty in which the tenants lived, these structures are not fondly remembered. Yet if they could be observed without knowledge of the economic condition of their inhabitants, the buildings would be seen as not bad-looking, and as possessing the elements of good design. Experiments in the Lower East Side and Harlem have shown these tenements can house up-to-date apartments. Such buildings appear better for the poor, psychologically as well as aesthetically, than the impersonal "vertical slums" favored by modern urban renewers.

New York, New York   *Richard Morris Hunt, Architect*
RESIDENCE OF MRS. WILLIAM B. ASTOR

Residence of Andrew Carnegie

New York, New York

Babb, Cook and Willard, *Architects*

Andrew Carnegie, the steel tycoon, is closely associated with Pittsburgh, but his two greatest houses were elsewhere. An immigrant to this country at twelve, he also loved his native Scotland, and in 1897 purchased as a summer residence an ancient castle named Skibo, which sits in Sutherland County in the northeast of that land. Carnegie considered New York City his American home throughout most of his life. When his steel company became U. S. Steel at the turn of the century, he retired from that field to devote himself to philanthropy. This business he managed from his new home, built in 1898-1900 to the designs of Babb, Cook, and Willard.

A fine Georgian mansion, impressive but not ostentatious, it had a rusticated first story of granite beneath a second and third story of brick, topped by a fourth floor recessed behind the cornice and balustrade. The structure continued through three more stories underground. A lawn and garden separated the house from the fence that bordered the pavement. (After being occupied for many years by the New York School of Social Work of Columbia University, the building is now the home of the Cooper-Hewitt Museum of Design.)

The house contained 64 rooms, many of which were generally too frilly to live up to the quality of the exterior. However, one room in particular should be noticed, since it so reveals the character of its patron. A man as interested in libraries as was Carnegie would be expected to have an especially grand one in his own house, and this was in fact the case. Around the top of the walls were scrolls bearing favorite adages Carnegie had collected throughout his life. As a young man, he had been invited to the Greensburg, Pennsylvania, home of Col. Niles A. Stokes, chief counsel for the Pennsylvania Railroad. Carved above the fireplace in Stokes's library was a book with an inscription that so impressed Carnegie that he wanted someday to have a similar arrangement in the library of a house of his own; eventually his Fifth Avenue mansion gave him that opportunity. The inscription read:

> He that cannot reason is a fool,
> He that will not is a bigot,
> He that dare not is a slave.

New York, New York　　　　　*Babb, Cook and Willard, Architects*
RESIDENCE OF ANDREW CARNEGIE

RESIDENCE OF RICHARD TOWNSEND—LIBRARY

RESIDENCE OF RICHARD TOWNSEND—HALL AND STAIRCASE

RESIDENCE OF RICHARD TOWNSEND—LIVING ROOM

RESIDENCE OF RICHARD TOWNSEND—BALLROOM

RESIDENCE OF RICHARD TOWNSEND—DINING ROOM

Residence of Miss Catherine Codman

Washington, District of Columbia

Ogden Codman, Jr., *Architect*

The delicacy and taste that belonged to a period maligned for clumsiness and clutter are well shown in the 1901 residence that Ogden Codman, Jr., designed for his cousin Catherine. A high, brick fence, crested by a balustrade, gives way to the court of a house with two protruding ells. The white marble ground level supports three red brick stories, including the attic. Among the fine decoration of the exterior are the shutters on all windows, the festoon plaques between the arched windows of the second story and the rectangular ones of the third, and the prominent quoins. The interiors are fully what would be expected of the architect who, together with Edith Wharton, wrote *The Decoration of Houses*, still the best American guide to interior decoration.

Miss Codman's summer home was the Berkeley Villa at Newport, a colonial-style house with French interiors; that residence, built in 1910, was, like the Washington mansion, designed by Ogden Codman, Jr. In 1928, at age 72, Miss Codman married Maxim Karolik, formerly a tenor with the Petrograd Opera, who was age 28. From all reports, their marriage was a very happy one. She died at ninety-two, and Karolik sold the house to Dwight Davis, then a member of the president's cabinet, who at the end of his stay in Washington sold the building to the Louise Home. Founded in 1869 by William W. Cochran in memory of his wife and daughter, both named Louise, the Home is a residence for pedigreed but impoverished ladies.

Washington, District of Columbia   *Ogden Codman, Jr., Architect*
RESIDENCE OF MISS CATHERINE CODMAN

Residence of Edward C. Knight

Philadelphia, Pennsylvania

Horace Trumbauer, *Architect*

A townhouse, as opposed to a mansion in the city, is built upon a narrow city lot and generally has dimensions equal to those of adjoining houses. Probably the most widely-known townhouses are the brownstones that the Romantic Era built, particularly in New York City. Today these are looked upon favorably, but because of nostalgia rather than architectural quality. Edith Wharton remembered "one of the most depressing impressions of my childhood" to be those houses with a "universal chocolate-coloured coating of the most hideous stone ever quarried," those "narrow houses so lacking in external dignity, so crammed with smug and suffocating upholstery." The Gilded Age replaced the brownstone facade with one of limestone or marble, and brought to the townhouse the dignity and refreshing airiness of classical architecture.

A fine example of a classical townhouse and of what classical design could do with the slimmest of lots is the residence Horace Trumbauer designed for Edward C. Knight. The slender facade contains at street level a door behind curving steps. The door leads to a passageway that connects with a reception room and the beautiful winding staircase that rises to the top floor. Because of the plot's tight squeeze, the facade has room for only a single window each on the first and second floors. These windows are highly decorated, and have handsome railings. The rooms behind the windows, being the living room on the first floor and the master bedroom on the second, are bright and sumptuously paneled. The elaborate entablature and cornice of the facade lead up to a balustrade, which carries four urns. Behind the balustrade rises a high mansard roof, with a single narrow window, lavishly framed.

The house, which was built in 1902, is carefully preserved as the headquarters of the Emergency Aid Society. Knight was so pleased with his French townhouse that he commissioned Trumbauer to design his Newport residence, Clarendon Court, an English mansion begun in 1903 and recently restored.

A variation on a townhouse is a rowhouse. A row of townhouses is usually a collection of buildings technically unattached and of different architects and designs, while a row of rowhouses is a block of residences, all of the same style and architect, and with party walls. The place where these buildings most abound is Philadelphia; a trip through that city's environs—the area between center city and the suburbs—will show row upon row upon row of rowhouses, built at about every time between the founding of the city and the present. These structures are both cause and result of the desire of the typical Philadelphian to own his own home, a characteristic that earned Philadelphia the title, The City of Homes.

Philadelphia, Pennsylvania   *Horace Trumbauer, Architect*

RESIDENCE OF EDWARD C. KNIGHT

Residence of E. M. Patterson

Washington, District of Columbia

McKim, Mead and White, *Architects*

The original plan for the city of Washington, designed in 1791-1792 by Maj. Pierre L'Enfant was a superb classical plan, fortunately reinforced by the McMillan Commission plan that came in 1902 at the height of the City Beautiful movement. Both plans scored the tedium of the grid plan, and instead favored an imaginative set of circles and rays, allées and closed axes. This arrangement created many nonrectangular pieces of real estate, whose challenge Gilded Age architects were both willing and equipped to meet, and met cleverly and beautifully.

Stanford White, of McKim, Mead and White,

met the problem of a site formed by the intersection of two streets at an angle somewhat less than 90 degrees. The instance was a residence for E. M. Patterson, publisher of the Washington *Times Herald*. The house was built in 1902, and is today the Washington Club.

Parallel to each street is an identical face. As each wing recedes from the street, they are linked by a center section that is at an equal angle to both wings. The center section continues the decoration of the sides, and contains the entrance, and a first-floor piazza that is topped by a balustrade to define a second-floor balcony.

The building's rooms are delicate and lovely, and give no credence to the lingering charges that the Gilded Age could not produce interiors as tasteful and dignified as those of any period in architectural history.

Washington, District of Columbia   *McKim, Mead and White, Architects*

RESIDENCE OF E. M. PATTERSON

RESIDENCE OF E. M. PATTERSON—SALON

Residence of E. M. Patterson—Library

Residence of Mrs. Isabella Stewart Gardner

Boston, Massachusetts

Edward H. Sears, *Architect*

True to the Boston virtue of a reserved exterior concealing whatever is within, the exterior of Fenway Court, the residence of Mrs. Isabella Stewart Gardner, is very plain, save for some details such as window frames from abroad. Inside, however, the house is anything but plain: it becomes a fabulous Venetian palace.

The house, for which Edward H. Sears was the architect, was completed in 1902 and occupied by Mrs. Gardner until her death in 1924. Isabella Stewart was born in New York City in 1840 of an aristocratic family. She and her husband, John Lowell Gardner, were both art collectors, an adventure Mrs.

Gardner continued after her husband's death in 1898. Her collecting was aided by the likes of Bernard Berenson, Charles Eliot Norton, and Joseph Lindon Smith. Her collection was essentially complete by 1916. Fenway Court, which overlooks the Fenway, a park system designed by Frederick Law Olmsted around 1878, was intended from its inception to serve eventually as an art museum, and so functions very well as the Isabella Stewart Gardner Museum.

The most important interior space is the center court, which rises through all four stories of the building to a glass roof. Decorated with mosaics and other works of art, the court is also richly planted. Guests today are admitted to three floors of galleries and the court they surround. Each room is interesting not only architecturally, but also for the marvelous collection.

Boston, Massachusetts   *Edward H. Sears, Architect*
RESIDENCE OF MRS. ISABELLA STEWART GARDNER

RESIDENCE OF MRS. ISABELLA STEWART GARDNER—COURT

]*44*[

Residence of Joseph Pulitzer
New York, New York

McKim, Mead and White, *Architects*

By 1900, most American architects had a firm grasp on the techniques of classicism, and were using them to turn out splendid buildings almost at will. This apparent ease of design is galling to the modernists with their emphasis on originality. But a vocabulary of basically fixed elements from which to pick and a basically fixed framework in which to arrange them has always been necessary in art. Mozart, Beethoven, and Schubert for example, selected from certain set musical elements, and placed them in a rather rigid framework to produce their symphonies. Yet those compositions are not at all repetitive or alike. Nor did this discipline reduce the individuality of a composer's work; the music of any one of the three men can readily be distinguished from that of the other two. But the discipline did produce beautiful music, which the supposed freedom of today's serious music does not. Likewise the discipline of classical architecture produced beautiful buildings, while the originality of modern architecture does not. And in art, beauty is the measure of success.

In looking at the New York City residence of Joseph Pulitzer, the newspaper publisher and originator of the Pulitzer Prize, it will be seen how well American architects, in this case McKim, Mead and White, had come to understand and use classicism by 1903.

A rusticated base bears, between a pair of square windows, three handsome grills that form the entrance. Identical first and second stories are lined with seven arched windows amidst an arrangement of engaged Ionic columns. Both floors are balustraded, and a third balustrade is above the cornice. A pitched roof with windows forms an attic.

The interiors are beautiful, but again beauty does not depend on originality. Probably the most unusual room is the round breakfast room, with its glass dome. All this room's elements, however, have appeared elsewhere before; still, the room, like the rest of the house, is one of a kind and has a personality all its own.

New York, New York   *McKim, Mead and White, Architects*
RESIDENCE OF JOSEPH PULITZER

]45[

RESIDENCE OF JOSEPH PULITZER—SECOND-STORY HALL

RESIDENCE OF JOSEPH PULITZER—BREAKFAST ROOM

Residence of James Buchanan Duke

New York, New York

Horace Trumbauer, *Architect*

For the New York City home of J. B. Duke, architect Horace Trumbauer designed a powerful building of deceptively uncomplicated elements, all perfectly proportioned in themselves and perfectly arranged among each other. The Fifth Avenue side contains lower and upper rows of four rectangular windows each and is crested by a balustrade. To that side of the building is joined by quoins the main facade, which is on Seventy-eighth Street. The same windows are here placed in two rows of six, divided into sets of three by a center section consisting of the entrance on the first story, the loggia holding Doric columns on the second, and the pediment, from the sides of which extends the balustrade.

Based on a Bordeaux mansion and erected in 1909-1911, the Duke residence is now the New York University Institute of Fine Arts. Duke was a great patron of Trumbauer, who also built for the tobacco millionaire his country house in Somerville, New Jersey, in those same three years, and altered his Newport cottage Rough Point in the 1920s. After Duke's death in 1925, Trumbauer designed two benefactions Duke had provided for: a small church, Duke's Chapel, built 1926, and nearly the entire campus of Duke University, built 1925 and thereafter, both at Durham, North Carolina.

New York, New York   *Horace Trumbauer, Architect*
RESIDENCE OF JAMES BUCHANAN DUKE

Residence of Henry Clay Frick
New York, New York
Carrere and Hastings, *Architects*

Beauty has come to be associated with the distant past: persons not familiar with the architecture of the Gilded Age are often surprised, on a visit to the Frick Collection, when they discover that the perfect setting for the splendid collection of Old Masters was built so recently as 1914. Originally the private home of Henry Clay Frick, who was the coke tycoon and a partner of Andrew Carnegie, the house was designed by Thomas Hastings of Carrere and Hastings.

The mansion stretches along the entire block front of Fifth Avenue between Seventieth and Seventy-first streets. The longest part of the facade consists of a rusticated first floor, and a smooth-walled second floor, tied together by two-story Ionic pilasters at the center of the facade. A plain third story, set behind a balustrade, held the servants' quarters. At the south

end of the facade is a two-story section, whose Seventieth Street side contains the present main entrance, which is crowned with a pediment containing sculpture by Sherry E. Fry. Extending from the other end of the Avenue facade is a long, very beautiful ell, terminating in a pavilion that also is favored with pedimental sculpture, this the work of Attilio Piccirilli. Behind the ell's colonnade is the west gallery, one of the many splendid interiors. The facade is set off from Fifth Avenue by a fence that also encloses a handsome garden.

Frick died in 1919, and his widow in 1931. In 1935, architect John Russell Pope converted the building from a private home to a museum of the works of art Frick had gathered. A carriageway became a spectacular interior court; the Oval Room, the East Gallery, and a round lecture hall were added.

The collection of art within the house is unquestionably one of the finest in the nation, but one's enjoyment of the collection is certainly increased by its surroundings.

New York, New York   *Carrere and Hastings, Architects*
RESIDENCE OF HENRY CLAY FRICK

Residence of Henry Clay Frick—Living Hall

Residence of Henry Clay Frick—West Gallery

Forest Hills Gardens

Forest Hills, New York

Grosvenor Atterbury and Others, *Architects*

The Russell Sage Foundation, a fund to improve social and living conditions, had no hesitation in stating that its housing development, Forest Hills Gardens, was a business venture aimed at profit. It was meant to be a middle-class area for people able to meet medium mortgage or rent payments (then considered to be about $25 a month). But in addition to a desire for fair financial gain, the Foundation also wanted to prove what could be done with a suburban housing project.

The Long Island Railroad had recently built a line through Forest Hills, a section in the New York City borough of Queens. There the firm of Frederick Law Olmsted laid out a tract of 142 acres, and in 1911 construction of the village began under chief architect Grosvenor Atterbury. Both town planning and architectural design followed the model of the garden cities of England. Atterbury designed the beautiful Station Square, which included the train station, an inn, a restaurant, stores, offices, and small apartments. Extending out from that point were winding streets between which were placed a great number of contiguous houses, many single dwellings,

as well as parks and playgrounds. Other than Atterbury, the architects for the project included Albro and Lindeburg, Wilson Eyre, J. T. Tubby, Jr., F. J. Sterner, Aymar Embury, and (in association with Atterbury) John A. Tompkins. Some lots were sold vacant, but the type of structure to be built was closely regulated by the development to see that the area retained a consistent flavor.

Forest Hills Gardens was a well-thought-out project. The residences were made small and reasonably priced, so that when the city expanded so as to envelop the community, the land values would not so increase as to cause large mansions to be torn down to release the valuable land upon which they sit. Though reasonably priced, the structures were extremely well built, so as to last and to require minimum maintenance. But the best aspect of the overall conception was the way the village looked. It remains largely intact today. Its message was heeded for a time in the construction of other projects across the country. If present-day developers really cared about how their tracts appeared to the eye, Forest Hills Gardens could continue to serve as an excellent prototype, but today's developers do not care in the least, nor do their architects, nor even, so it seems, their prospects; such crimes as Levittown, further out on Long Island from Forest Hills, now look attractive next to the housing projects of today.

· GROUP · XXXIII ·
· TWO · DETACHED · AND · FOUR · BLOCK · HOUSES ·

Forest Hills, New York   *Grosvenor Atterbury, Architect*
FOREST HILLS GARDENS—"TWO DETACHED AND FOUR BLOCK HOUSES"

FOREST HILLS GARDENS—RESIDENCE OF MARK LAWSON

3
Country Estates

The Gilded Age opened the countryside to convenient living for many people for the first time. Country life had before been confined to people who lived and worked there, such as farmers, and to people who could get away from the city for long enough periods to make the lengthy trip worthwhile, such as the rich who did not work. Of course, before the population expansion of the Gilded Age the cities were much smaller, and a reasonably rural scene could be achieved by a short carriage ride. But with the Gilded Age's favorite industry, the railroads, came the possibilities for large estates set in genuine countryside. While many of these country seats are now in the innermost suburbs, they were, when new, in wide open spaces, or at least spaces as wide open as their civilized tenants wanted them to be.

The palatial homes that the rich built in the suburbs are probably the greatest and most typical of the Gilded Age's contributions to architecture. They are also the most wantonly destroyed. The drop in the standard of living since 1929 made their use as residences seemingly obsolete, but they are still eminently practical for museums, offices, and so on. Nevertheless, a large number of them are abandoned, sacked by suburban vandals (that is, the children of "good" homes), and eventually demolished for tract home developments. By its country estates, the Gilded Age is remembered. The present age will be remembered for tearing them down.

Residence of Thomas Alva Edison
West Orange, New Jersey
Henry Hudson Holly, *Architect*

Glenmont was built in 1880 for Henry C. Pedder, manager of the New York City firm of Arnold Constable and Company, which later found it necessary to take over the title to the house. In 1886, it was purchased from the company by Thomas Alva Edison, the inventor and authentic American genius. Edison and his second wife moved into the house soon after their marriage in that year; they occupied it until their deaths, his in 1931, hers 16 years later. The house has been a National Historic Site since 1955, and is open to the public. Visitors will also want to inspect Llewellyn Park as a whole; this is the private park containing Glenmont and other fine homes and gardens. Edison's laboratories, to which in 1887 he transferred his operations from Menlo Park, are also on view.

The mansion is eminently Victorian, a fine example of that style's grand products then being built in the suburbs. A basement of bluestone blocks from Greenwich, Connecticut, supports a first story of pressed brick from Baltimore, trimmed with Wyoming firestone, above which the second and third stories of half-timber construction rise to a slate roof. The massing of the house is coherent, save for the second-floor living room, which seems out of place above the porte-cochère. This room's interior also seems to be apart from the elegance of the rest of the residence: the Edisons always regarded the room of books, memorabilia, and family photographs as their retreat. The search for grandeur does not much increase in the second floor's five bedrooms, but it does downstairs, as seen in the drawing room, the dining room, and even the conservatory. Most grand is the foyer, with its red mahogany staircase that epitomizes the design concepts set forth in the published writings and drawings of the house's architect, Henry Hudson Holly.

West Orange, New Jersey   Henry Hudson Holly, *Architect*
RESIDENCE OF THOMAS ALVA EDISON

RESIDENCE OF THOMAS ALVA EDISON—LIVING ROOM

RESIDENCE OF THOMAS ALVA EDISON—CONSERVATORY

RESIDENCE OF THOMAS ALVA EDISON—FOYER AND STAIRCASE

Residence of Charles A. Potter

Philadelphia, Pennsylvania

Wilson Eyre, Jr., *Architect*

Philadelphia, which has always had a passion for suburban living, readily adopted the shingle style, which offered both refinement and rambling comfort. In that style, on a corner lot in Chestnut Hill, within the city limits but retaining to this day a suburban feeling, was built in 1881-1882 the Charles A. Potter house Anglecot, designed by Wilson Eyre, Jr.

Heavily influenced, as was much shingle style architecture at that time, by the Newport Casino (shown later in this volume), the residence takes on the club's brick first story, wide, central arch, and richly decorated gable within a larger, plainer one; the clock from the Casino's court becomes a sundial on Anglecot's facade. The residence's rooms are delicately decorated, much of the interior ornament being supplied by walls and ceilings, as well as such features as the staircase.

Today, despite some clumsy recent additions, the house can be seen about as when new. It now contains the Anglecot Sanatorium. Philadelphia's admiration for the shingle style kept the area building in this rural style long after most other places had abandoned it for the more formal classicism.

Philadelphia, Pennsylvania   *Wilson Eyre, Jr., Architect*
RESIDENCE OF CHARLES A. POTTER

Residence of Pierre Lorillard

Tuxedo Park, New York

Bruce Price, *Architect*

In the mid-1880s, Pierre Lorillard began to build Tuxedo Park, a wealthy community within commuting distance from New York City and a simpler alternative to Newport. The chief planner and architect was Bruce Price. His finished product was very successful architecturally, although it tended to lack the interest of a town that grew gradually: Julia Ward Howe called it the "white of an egg." Tuxedo Park was also successful socially: it gave its name to the new, more informal menswear. The final decision between the two then-current names, the other being the Newport, was probably made by Emily Post, the daughter of Bruce Price.

This house, the residence of J. L. Breese for many years although one of several houses Lorillard owned in the community, clearly shows the simplicity of early Tuxedo Park architecture. In search of simplicity, Price reduced the house to its functional necessities, thereby anticipating modern building. Whatever beauty the house possesses derives mainly from its shape, especially that provided by the pair of brick chimneys. The Gilded Age was not to be denied its decoration, however, and more elaborate residences soon began to appear at Tuxedo Park.

Tuxedo Park, New York   *Bruce Price, Architect*

RESIDENCE OF PIERRE LORILLARD

Residence of George W. Vanderbilt

Asheville, North Carolina

Richard Morris Hunt, *Architect*

The desire for empire among the Gilded Age wealthy produced many unusual results, none more unusual than the Biltmore estate in Asheville, North Carolina. There, George Washington Vanderbilt set up a democratized version of a feudal kingdom. The estate was for the most part self-supporting, and covered 125,000 acres of farmland, woods, and mountains. The grounds were laid out by Frederick Law Olmsted, who is most famous for designing Central Park in New York City.

The French Renaissance mansion by Richard Morris Hunt was opened in 1895. It is closely related in style to the Fifth Avenue mansion that the same architect had designed over a decade earlier for George W. Vanderbilt's older brother, W. K. Vanderbilt (a house shown in the previous chapter), as well as to Ochre Court, the summer residence of Ogden Goelet, with which in 1891 the same architect had introduced a full-fledged Gilded Age palace to Newport and resort communities at large. Containing 250 rooms, Biltmore is the largest of the three mansions; still, the intricate detailing of the exterior is not overwhelmed by the size of the walls.

Just past the entrance hall is the grand staircase; a reverse copy of the staircase at the Chateau de Blois, the staircase shows no support on its inside edge. The wrought-iron chandelier that hangs in the stairwell is thought to be the world's largest that is suspended from a single point.

In the Palm Court, plants grown on the estate are displayed. From the wooden ribs that support the glass ceiling hang eighteenth-century Italian lanterns of brass. At the center of the marble floor stands a fountain; its statue of boy and swan is by Karl Bitter.

An especially impressive room of state is the banquet hall, which is 42 by 72 feet beneath a 75-foot arched ceiling. Karl Bitter's carving, *The Return from the Chase,* crowns the massive triple fireplace. Beneath the organ gallery are characters from Wagner's operas, these figures also by Bitter. The ability of that sculptor, however, is best shown here in the statues of St. Louis and especially Joan of Arc, both above the banquet hall entrance.

The library ceiling, imported from an Italian palace on the promise the previous owner's name would never be revealed, is attributed to Pellegrini. It looks down on spectacular Circassian walnut woodwork, including a marvelous spiral staircase.

Mr. Vanderbilt's baronial bedroom, paneled in walnut, contrasts with Mrs. Vanderbilt's lighter, oval bedroom, whose walls are covered with yellow Scalamandre silk.

The mansion is splendidly furnished with antiques and with pieces made for the house. The contents of the Tapestry Gallery alone would fascinate the art connoisseur (and the view from the Tapestry Gallery loggia do the same for the naturalist). A good deal of the collecting for the mansion was accomplished by Vanderbilt himself. He was, incidentally, in his twenties when work on Biltmore was begun.

Since 1930, the mansion and its gardens have been open to the public: one of the best Gilded Age estates became one of the first to become a museum of itself. The grounds have by today been reduced to a mere 11,000 acres, but sufficient land has been turned into a national forest to insure the idyllic vistas.

Asheville, North Carolina   *Richard Morris Hunt, Architect*
RESIDENCE OF GEORGE W. VANDERBILT

RESIDENCE OF GEORGE W. VANDERBILT—BANQUET HALL

RESIDENCE OF GEORGE W. VANDERBILT—STAIRCASE

]60[

RESIDENCE OF GEORGE W. VANDERBILT—TAPESTRY GALLERY

RESIDENCE OF GEORGE W. VANDERBILT—LIBRARY

RESIDENCE OF GEORGE W. VANDERBILT—OAK DRAWING ROOM

RESIDENCE OF GEORGE W. VANDERBILT—MR. VANDERBILT'S BEDROOM

RESIDENCE OF GEORGE W. VANDERBILT—MRS. VANDERBILT'S BEDROOM

Residence of Frederick W. Vanderbilt

Hyde Park, New York

McKim, Mead and White, *Architects*

Frederick W. Vanderbilt, son of William Henry Vanderbilt, had hired Charles Follen McKim, of McKim, Mead and White, to enlarge a newly-acquired country home, the Langdon mansion at Hyde Park, a Greek residence built in 1847. True to the Vanderbilt passion to build, this idea was soon abandoned, and the Langdon house was demolished, and in 1896-1898 replaced by a splendid new country mansion.

Each elevation of the mansion has a portico: a squared porch at the entrance front and at each of the building's ends, and a curved porch at the rear. The portico's composite columns rise next to the first two stories of the rectangular structure, which is topped by an attic with cresting balustrade.

Behind the carefully conceived exteriors are fine rooms by decorators Ogden Codman, Jr., and George A. Glaenzer. Many furnishings came from Napoleon's chateau at Malmaison, near Paris. The ceiling of the drawing room was painted by muralist H. Siddons Mowbray; the painting never appealed to the Vanderbilts and was removed in 1906 when architect Whitney Warren redecorated the room and made other interior changes in the house.

While the mansion was under construction, the Vanderbilts occupied a pavilion built in 66 days on the former site of a carriage house. The pavilion is in itself a fine mansion, with widow's walk and with Doric portico supporting a pediment. After the completion of the big house, the Vanderbilts still occupied the house during winter weekends when they came out from their New York City residence, and to contain the overflow of guests when the rooms of the main building were full.

The gardener's cottage and the tool house antedate Vanderbilt ownership of the grounds; these buildings were erected in 1875 from the plans of John H. Sturgis and Charles Brigham, Boston architects, for former owner Walter Langdon. The 1897 coach house by R. H. Robertson was redesigned by him in 1910 to also accommodate automobiles. The main and river gatehouses and gates were designed by McKim, Mead and White, and constructed in 1898. The estate covered a considerably larger area during the Vanderbilt occupancy, and a number of other outbuildings beyond the present boundaries are now in private hands.

The Vanderbilt mansion is one of that small group of Gilded Age country mansions—or, for that matter, Gilded Age residences of any kind—that are displayed for their own sake. There should be many more. Current preservation forces tend to think colonial houses more worthy of maintaining, since they seem more historic. But the Gilded Age is certainly as historically important as any period in the nation's life, and the original owners of the period's great residences were certainly among the era's most important figures. Gilded Age mansions, when they become unoccupied, can be opened to the public by private societies, or by municipal, state, or federal government: the Vanderbilt mansion is under the care of the National Park Service. To guard against the future, the lifesaving title National Historic Landmark or its local equivalent should be given to many Gilded Age buildings whether or not still in use; whole districts of mansions, such as those groups at Elkins Park, Pennsylvania, and Newport, Rhode Island, should receive such distinction. The best Gilded Age structures of all types, not only residences, should be safeguarded. Gilded Age buildings are among America's most endangered species.

RESIDENCE OF FREDERICK W. VANDERBILT—PAVILION

Residence of George W. Elkins

Elkins Park, Pennsylvania

Horace Trumbauer, *Architect*

As were most styles of English derivation, Tudor, a development of the Gothic, was highly popular during the Gilded Age. One American adaptation, mainly found in smaller houses, was a Tudor simply suggested by such features as half-timber construction, a style Eero Saarinen cleverly labeled "pseudor-Tudor." Other buildings, however, were built in a very correct Tudor: one of these structures was Chelten House.

A high terrace, walled by stone, spreads beneath the main section of the house, which is of three stories, including that whose dormers penetrate the roof. At one end, the main section is joined at an obtuse angle to a two-story service wing. A dramatic porte-cochère is at the other end. The mansion's interiors use a fittingly large number of plaster relief ceilings and of walls paneled in dark wood. A vast bay window on one front illuminates the two-story great hall; on the other front, a smaller bay window lights the main staircase. An especially charming exterior feature is the many grotesques, which are also found on the beautiful, flowing stables, whose style matches that of the mansion.

Chelten House was built in 1896, the stable in 1899, a small casino, also Tudor, in 1904, and a large fountain in 1906; the mansion was destroyed by fire in 1908 and rebuilt in the following year. Now a Dominican retreat house for women, it was built

originally for George W. Elkins, son of William L. Elkins, the traction magnate, for whom was named Elkins Park, the town where Chelten House is located.

Elkins Park, just north of Philadelphia, was the central community in and around which the new wealthy of the Gilded Age built their grand homes. This area, earlier called Shoemakertown or Ogontz, was chosen by the millionaires partly for its great natural beauty, as was Roslyn, Long Island, which is to New York City as Elkins Park is to Philadelphia. The addition of Gilded Age mansions made these towns even more certainly their city's most beautiful suburb. Most of Elkins Park's large mansions, as well as many of its smaller houses, were designed by Horace Trumbauer, the best architect Philadelphia has produced. Among his bigger mansions in Elkins Park and vicinity, along with Chelten House, are Gray Towers, the residence of William Welsh Harrison, built in 1892, now Beaver College; Elstowe, the residence of William L. Elkins, built in 1898, now part of the Dominican retreat; Lynnewood, the residence of P. A. B. Widener, built in 1898-1900, now Faith Theological Seminary (a structure illustrated later in this chapter); the residence of Sidney F. Tyler, built in 1912-1914, now Tyler Art School; Ronaele Manor, the residence of F. Eugene Dixon, built in 1923-1926, now unoccupied; and Whitemarsh Hall, the residence of Edward T. Stotesbury, built in 1916-1920, now unoccupied (shown in this book's last chapter). Happily, all these buildings are still standing.

Elkins Park, Pennsylvania   *Horace Trumbauer, Architect*

RESIDENCE OF GEORGE W. ELKINS

Residence of Lloyd Bryce

Roslyn, New York

Ogden Codman, Jr., *Architect*

Of all the suburbs of New York City, the town that attracted the greatest number of the wealthy and their country estates was Roslyn, Long Island. Although it is still a good area in which to live, many of the Gilded Age mansions there have been torn down. One of those still standing was built around 1896 for Lloyd Bryce, minister to Luxembourg and the Netherlands, and later the owner and editor of *North American Review*. After Bryce's death in 1917, the house was bought by Childs Frick, palaeontologist and son of Henry Clay Frick, the coke magnate. Childs Frick employed Sir Charles Carrick Allom of London to rebuild the house; the alterations were few without and many within. Upon the death of Frick in 1965, Nassau County, in which the estate stands, purchased most of the stately grounds to create the William Cullen Bryant Nature Preserve, named for the poet and Roslyn resident, who owned part of the land that became Bryce's.

Recently, the mansion became the Nassau County Art Museum.

From the entrance front, the house appears to be a rectangular block, consisting of two brick stories with quoins beneath a roof bearing dormers. At the garden front, however, a curved, one-story wing extends from each end of the center block to terminate in a pavilion. Both wings and the first floor of the center section have round-arched doors on the garden side; a balcony, which partway crosses the center section, divides the first story from the second, which has shuttered, rectangular windows. The balance of the Georgian style is equaled by the balance between heavy and light, imposing and playful that the skillful architect, Ogden Codman, Jr., gave the house.

The mansion overlooks Hempstead Harbor, and the views inside the house are beautiful, too. Codman believed the architect of a house should also be its interior decorator. A house as a whole should be simple and functional, a "mechanism for living." Such sentiments seem modern, until it is realized that Codman rejected asymmetry and the theories that led to modernism and thought classical design the simplest, most functional, and most beautiful.

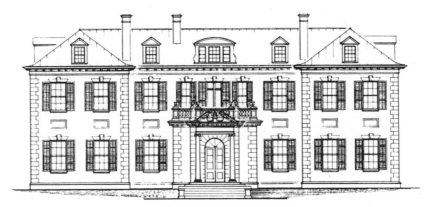

Roslyn, New York   *Ogden Codman, Jr., Architect*

RESIDENCE OF LLOYD BRYCE
In a drawing by the architect.

RESIDENCE OF LLOYD BRYCE—GARDEN FRONT

RESIDENCE OF LLOYD BRYCE—DRAWING ROOM

RESIDENCE OF LLOYD BRYCE—DINING ROOM

Residence of Giraud Foster

Lenox, Massachusetts

Carrere and Hastings, *Architects*

Bellefontaine, built in 1897 for Giraud Foster, is the finest of Carrere and Hastings's country mansions, certainly a distinguished field to lead. Adding to the house's own excellence is the beauty of the surrounding Berkshires.

The brick and marble mansion does not possess the high roof often found on residences by those architects, but the structure does exhibit the characteristic verticality of their designs. On the entrance front is a spectacular portico of two-story Corinthian columns. At the ends of the building are pavilions with round arches. These extend back to surround both sides of the garden front terrace and its fine fountain. At the rear of the house, the third story becomes evident, although it was concealed on the entrance front. The interiors, including the Louis XIII living room, and the dining room and salon, both Louis XV, are worthy of this great home.

The building still stands and is now the Immaculate Heart of Mary Seminary.

Lenox, Massachusetts   *Carrere and Hastings, Architects*
RESIDENCE OF GIRAUD FOSTER

RESIDENCE OF GIRAUD FOSTER—GARDEN FRONT

RESIDENCE OF GIRAUD FOSTER—PERGOLA AND FOUNTAIN

RESIDENCE OF GIRAUD FOSTER—LIVING ROOM

RESIDENCE OF GIRAUD FOSTER—DINING ROOM

RESIDENCE OF GIRAUD FOSTER—PARLOR

Residence of Stanford White

St. James, New York

Stanford White, *Architect*

The exercise of looking at the homes of the architects themselves is not always as revealing as might be imagined. Since the architects did not always have as much money as their clients, they therefore could not afford the architectural possibilities offered to customers. But Stanford White, of McKim, Mead and White, had lots of money. He had a house on Gramercy Park in New York City, although he preferred to live when in town at his apartment in nearby Madison Square Garden, which was his favorite of all the buildings he designed (and which is shown later in this volume). He also had a country residence at St. James, Long Island, a house he designed for himself in the 1890s. To this day, it remains in the hands of his family.

The ends of three gables are presented at the third story of the St. James facade. The second floor has shuttered windows, and a piazza crosses the first story. The exterior of the house is not elaborate, but it is a relaxed introduction to the informal —and unique—interiors. The living room was decorated with a rich collection of diverse elements wonderfully arranged into a whole. The extensive use of glass brilliantly illuminates the dining room, which contains clutter more prosaic than that of the living room.

This host of decorations spills over to the estate's grounds, whose plantings are equally varied. A prominent garden decoration was a reduced-size model of Augustus St. Gaudens's *Diana* that crowned Madison Square Garden. The house and grounds can be seen as a summary of White's design: beautiful, simple shapes, decorated with much careful, complicated ornament.

St. James, New York   *Stanford White, Architect*

RESIDENCE OF STANFORD WHITE

RESIDENCE OF STANFORD WHITE—LIVING ROOM

RESIDENCE OF STANFORD WHITE—DINING ROOM

Residence of C. Ledyard Blair

Bernardsville, New Jersey

Carrere and Hastings, *Architects*

When the time had come for the Gilded Age to build its largest and most impressive mansions, they appeared almost overnight. Compare the first building in the chapter, Glenmont, the Edison house in West Orange, New Jersey, with Blairsden, built for C. Ledyard Blair at nearby Bernardsville. The Edison mansion is large for its day, random in its planning, derived from the quaint Queen Anne style. The Blair mansion is huge by any standards, formal in its design, and based on the more exacting Louis XIII style. And yet Blairsden was erected in 1898, only 18 years after the building of Glenmont.

Blairsden rests upon a terrace that is retained by stone walls. The third and fourth stories are contained within a high roof. Such a roof contributes to the verticality usually found in the buildings of Carrere and Hastings, Blairsden's architects. This identifying characteristic is also to be seen in the pairing of first- and second-floor doors and windows within unique two-story versions of the Gibbs surround.

The interiors were appropriately grand. The Italian walnut paneling of the library was certainly more traditional than that of Glenmont. Nevertheless, Blairsden displayed a touch of earlier taste: the living room was old-fashionedly furnished with the decorations from an old house on Second Avenue, New York City.

Bernardsville, New Jersey   *Carrere and Hastings, Architects*
RESIDENCE OF C. LEDYARD BLAIR

RESIDENCE OF C. LEDYARD BLAIR—ENCLOSED GARDEN AND PERGOLA

RESIDENCE OF C. LEDYARD BLAIR—LIVING ROOM

Residence of Henry W. Poor

Tuxedo Park, New York

T. Henry Randall, *Architect*

At Tuxedo Park, founded as a simpler community for the wealthy, the residential land had been divided into small plots. This did not stop Henry W. Poor from crowding onto one of them a house of true Gilded Age size and splendor.

The house is Jacobean, a style characterized by the curved ends it places on its gables. The windows in the Jacobean tend to be large, and the Poor mansion continues this quality in its loggias. Jacobean in as pure a form as this was not all that widely built in the United States, but, had it been, there is doubt this residence would ever have been surpassed; few Jacobean structures in the style's native England can boast such wonderful features as the carving at the entrance.

The unusual exterior surrounds a number of unusual interiors. The most eccentric room is the smoke room, with its pictures, mounted heads, tankards, and high fireplace mantel.

The mansion's original owner, Henry W. Poor, had a city house on Gramercy Park; he was a Wall Street speculator and the originator of *Poor's Manual of Securities*. When in the late 1890s his Tuxedo Park mansion was reaching completion, Henry M. Tilford, president of Standard Oil of Ohio, said he would like to buy the Jacobean structure should ever Poor decide to sell. Poor, realizing the nature of his own business, also realized he would want to sell quickly should his investments prove bad. He told Tilford he would give the oilman the first chance to buy the house should it go on the market, if Tilford could produce, within 24 hours of the decision to sell, a certified check for one-half million dollars. Tilford agreed. Not long after, Poor was forced to sell the mansion, and, shortly before ten one morning, he advised Tilford of the decision. The check reached Poor's office at 11:15 the same morning. The arrangement designed to keep Poor from the poorhouse also made Tilford the owner of one.

Tuxedo Park, New York   *T. Henry Randall, Architect*

RESIDENCE OF HENRY W. POOR

RESIDENCE OF HENRY W. POOR—ENTRANCE

RESIDENCE OF HENRY W. POOR—PORCH

RESIDENCE OF HENRY W. POOR—LIBRARY

RESIDENCE OF HENRY W. POOR—SMOKE ROOM

Residence of P. A. B. Widener

Elkins Park, Pennsylvania

Horace Trumbauer, *Architect*

The question of livability often comes up when people from the present contemplate mansions from the Gilded Age. A tourist passing through a tremendous banquet hall wonders how a solitary diner eating a cup of soup kept from feeling lonely or at least timid in such a room. The Gilded Age was not much on timidity, and loneliness can also be felt in the smallest hotel room. Most of the Gilded Age wealthy, in fact, did not live in these spectacular rooms, but used them only on special occasions. Everyday living in their large country estates was done in private apartments. The bedrooms of these estates, it will be noticed, are generally small proportionately, although usually larger than the average bedroom today, and certainly more elaborate. In such more restrained quarters, a more typical family life was possible.

Even such palaces as Lynnewood Hall, built for P. A. B. Widener in Elkins Park, Pennsylvania, was designed for practical living. Widener had built in center-city Philadelphia in 1886 a Victorian mansion (seen earlier herein) that housed the traction magnate, his wife, his two grown sons, their wives and children, and the family art collection. Even that large house was soon overflowing, and so Horace Trumbauer was commissioned to plan a 110-room mansion just north of Philadelphia to hold the family and its art.

Trumbauer gave the house a long front section and a wing extending back from the center of that section. The rooms of state needed for lavish entertaining were placed across the first floor of the front section. The second floor of that section was divided basically into two private apartments, one for one son, his family, and his widowed father, the other for the other son and his family. The wing at the rear was devoted to the art galleries. These were lighted from the top, allowing the windows on the sides of the wing to light the servants' rooms, which were so many as to make their corridors resemble those of a hotel. The building's three divisions meet in a great hall, which in design seems to continue indoors the magnificently austere classical facade through which the hall is reached.

The estate, onto which the family moved in 1900, grew to include a number of fine smaller buildings on extensive grounds. A dairy farm was present, as well as facilities for raising and training horses. An entire racetrack on the estate bore witness to the Widener passion for horseflesh, a love that later manifested itself in the family's development of Belmont Park, Elmont, New York, for which Trumbauer designed grandstand and other buildings during the 1920s.

A few years after the completion of Lynnewood, the landscaping was improved by Jacques Greber and to the mansion was added pedimental sculpture on the facade and an extension of the rear wing to include on the upper floor a special room for the art collection's Van Dyck paintings, and on the first floor an interior diving tank.

After the death in 1912 of the eldest son, George D. Widener, and in 1915 of the father, the other son, Joseph Widener, maintained the house as a single mansion until 1941, when the estate was deserted. He gave the art collection to the National Gallery of Art, Washington (which is the last shown in this book); one of the largest parts of that museum's collection, the Widener painting and sculpture first went on display there in 1942. Lynnewood Hall was empty to 1952, when it was purchased by Faith Theological Seminary, which occupies it today. The grounds outside the wrought-iron fence that surrounds the mansion were sold separately and are now occupied mainly by garden apartments and a shopping center.

Elkins Park, Pennsylvania   *Horace Trumbauer, Architect*
RESIDENCE OF P. A. B. WIDENER

RESIDENCE OF P. A. B. WIDENER—SIDE VIEW

RESIDENCE OF P. A. B. WIDENER—GREAT HALL

RESIDENCE OF P. A. B. WIDENER—DINING ROOM

RESIDENCE OF P. A. B. WIDENER—ART GALLERY

RESIDENCE OF P. A. B. WIDENER—AERIAL VIEW

The small building near the top of the picture is one of the estate's stables. The mansion to the extreme right is Ogontz, which that pioneer tycoon, banker Jay Cooke built soon after the Civil War; on the site of the house now stands Ronaele Manor.

Residence of A. Cass Canfield

Roslyn, New York

McKim, Mead and White, *Architects*

In building the Roslyn residence in 1902 for A. Cass Canfield, McKim, Mead and White produced their best Georgian country house. A three- story center section separates a pair of two-story wings, all balanced about a magnificent entranceway. More animated than the entrance front is the garden front: a vast bay projects onto terrace. Through the bay is the living room, paneled in French walnut. The library is lined with oak and has its windows and bookcases set within round arches.

Roslyn, New York　　　　　　　*McKim, Mead and White, Architects*
RESIDENCE OF A. CASS CANFIELD

RESIDENCE OF A. CASS CANFIELD—LIVING ROOM

RESIDENCE OF A. CASS CANFIELD—LIBRARY

Residence of Clarence H. Mackay
Roslyn, New York
McKim, Mead and White, *Architects*

American aristocracy, being an artificial one within a democracy, found it necessary to maintain a high snub rate, so that it would be clear who was better than who. Louise Mackay, wife of John Mackay who had made his millions from the Comstock Lode, was repeatedly snubbed when she tried to enter New York society. Her family was not to be admitted until her son, Clarence H. Mackay, married Katherine Alexander Duer, of an honorable New York lineage. John Mackay offered his new daughter-in-law whatever wedding gift she wanted; she asked for the finest estate on Long Island. Soon Stanford White was commissioned to design the mansion which was at Roslyn, overlooking Hempstead Bay, and was called Harbor Hill.

The facade of Harbor Hill was really too severe, but it was relieved in the carving of the main entrance door and the dormers. The great hall was paneled in oak, and contained oak columns and pilasters. The library, where tapestries shared the walls with a dado below a green-striped covering, was filled with live flowers, as was, of course, the conservatory. The plasterwork in the white drawing room was spectacular.

The estate's stable, designed by Warren and Wetmore, was without doubt worthy of that catchall word for Gilded Age architecture, "eclecticism."

Completed in 1902, the mansion was demolished in the 1940s to make way for smaller, upper-class homes. In the time between, Harbor Hill was the scene of many social triumphs for the now enfranchised Mackays. Probably the greatest victory was on 7 September 1924, when they entertained there the Prince of Wales (who later became the Duke of Windsor). Present was the 81-year-old Louise Mackay, who society had so snubbed years before.

Roslyn, New York   *McKim, Mead and White, Architects*
RESIDENCE OF CLARENCE H. MACKAY

RESIDENCE OF CLARENCE H. MACKAY—WHITE DRAWING ROOM

RESIDENCE OF CLARENCE H. MACKAY—MRS. MACKAY'S BATHROOM

Warren and Wetmore, Architects
RESIDENCE OF CLARENCE H. MACKAY—STABLE

Residence of Mrs. Phoebe A. Hearst

Pleasanton, California

A. C. Schweinfurth, *Architect*

The houses built in California during the Gilded Age were sometimes in the romantic or traditional styles then popular in the East, but more often were in more native styles. These derived from the architecture of Spain, the overall Mediterranean, Florida, or even, the shingle style being influential, the Northeast. Hacienda del Pozo de Verona, the Pleasanton residence of Mrs. Phoebe A. Hearst, drew from the buildings of Mexico.

The house, built in 1903 from the design of A. C. Schweinfurth, is almost unornamented and depends for its appearance on its shape. The structure has thick walls made of cement. In the Mexican tradition, a central court separates the main dwelling section of the house from the lower section for servants. At the center of the courtyard stands the well head from Verona for which the mansion (House of the Well of Verona) was named. Like the exterior, the rooms of the hacienda are basically plain, and rely on their vivid furnishings for distinction.

The wife of U. S. senator from California George Hearst and the mother of newspaper publisher William Randolph Hearst, Phoebe Apperson Hearst, who was born in 1842 and died in 1919, was known in her own right as a philanthropist. The mansion served as the clubhouse of the Castlewood Country Club from its founding in 1926 to the building's destruction by fire in August 1969.

Pleasanton, California   *A. C. Schweinfurth, Architect*
RESIDENCE OF MRS. PHOEBE A. HEARST

RESIDENCE OF MRS. PHOEBE A. HEARST—MUSIC ROOM

RESIDENCE OF MRS. PHOEBE A. HEARST—LIBRARY

4
Resort Cottages

*R*esort cottages were special in the realm of Gilded Age architecture: they were the special province of the wealthy. Although anyone might own a little house in city or country, and although a person whose job was at a resort might own a year-round home there, an actual resort cottage—a second home at a place distant from one's business—and the time to enjoy the cottage could only be had by the rich, or at least the well-to-do.

This exclusiveness being the case, the rich could democratically call their resort houses "cottages," even though the edifices often ran to 75 rooms. But there the thought of equality ended: each family strove to outdo the next in the splendor of their cottage. Since the cottages were meant for use only a short time each year—the Newport season lasted only six weeks, from the middle of July to the end of August—they could be built smaller than corresponding country estates, and since the cottages were meant for use only on holiday, they could be fancifully designed. The results were lavish, fanciful, relatively smaller structures: the jewels of Gilded Age architecture.

Kragsyde: Summer Residence
of G. Nixon Black

Manchester-by-the-Sea, Massachusetts

Peabody and Stearns, *Architects*

The shingle style is well suited to resort sites. It is a relief from the formality of city and country architecture. At the resorts, nature can be appreciated for a stay, and the shingle style house sits with natural ease near trees, rocks, and waves, but never goes so far as to pretend to "blend in" with its surroundings, the state for which modern architects hanker.

Upon the rocks of Manchester-by-the-Sea, Massachusetts, and overlooking the Atlantic Ocean, is Kragsyde, built around 1882 for G. Nixon Black from the designs of Peabody and Stearns. The informality of the shingle style allowed the rooms to be placed in the free arrangement seen in the plan. For instance, the library, which a piazza surrounds on a back wing set at a 45-degree angle to the front section of the house, is on a level between the parlor and bedroom levels. An architect working in the shingle style could pick whatever elements he wanted —in the case of Kragsyde, such elements as bays, piazzas, dormers, towers, and a driveway arch— then arrange them freely, and cover the whole with a blanket of shingles.

Manchester-by-the-Sea, Massachusetts   *Peabody and Stearns, Architects*
KRAGSYDE: SUMMER RESIDENCE OF G. NIXON BLACK

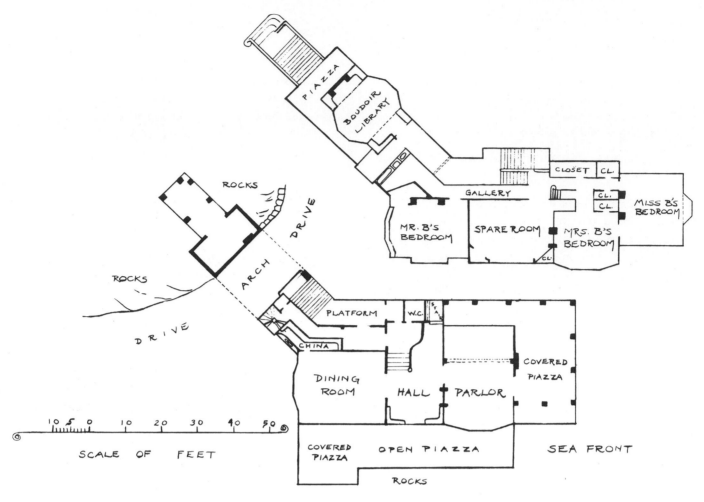

KRAGSYDE: SUMMER RESIDENCE OF G. NIXON BLACK—PLAN

Ochre Point: Summer Residence of Robert Goelet

Newport, Rhode Island

McKim, Mead and White, *Architects*

The Gilded Age as it gained momentum began to envision itself in surroundings grander than the shingle style was able to provide. Ochre Point, also called Southside, dates from 1882-1883, when the shingle style was a major style for construction at the best resorts; the house was built for Robert Goelet, a prominent member of New York society, and stands to this day overlooking the Atlantic Ocean across the Cliff Walk in Newport, the Gilded Age's most heady resort. For such an owner and location, the rustic shingle style found itself gaining cosmopolitan classicizing aspects.

Instead of the random placement of elements in Kragsyde (the previous building illustrated), much symmetry, a mark of the classical, is to be discovered in Ochre Point. On the street side, two semicircular bays—that on the left holding the library, that on the right the main staircase—sit symmetrically about a piazza, at which the entrance stairs, if not the front door, are symmetrically arranged. Facing the sea, a piazza projects two gables symmetrically. The north wing, which would appear to throw off the symmetry of the whole, is actually the service wing, leaving the main section of the house to give a basically symmetrical image.

Decoration, normally present on the exteriors of classical structures, but seldom to be seen on those of shingle style buildings, returns in the plaster panels by Stanford White. These give a foretaste of what he was to achieve in the decoration of later buildings such as the Century Association and Madison Square Garden (both of which are shown later in this book).

Although the cottage is certainly handsome and represents a step toward the grandeur the Gilded Age at its height was to require of its architecture, the shingle style was only capable of going so far in that direction before having to concede supremacy to the classical.

Newport, Rhode Island   *McKim, Mead and White, Architects*
OCHRE POINT: SUMMER RESIDENCE OF ROBERT GOELET

OCHRE POINT: SUMMER RESIDENCE OF ROBERT GOELET—GREAT HALL

Summer Residence of William Low

Bristol, Rhode Island

McKim, Mead and White, *Architects*

By the end of the 1880s, classicism had surpassed the shingle style as the current building style, even at the resorts. One of the last efforts by McKim, Mead and White in the shingle style was made in 1887 in the William Low house at Bristol, a Rhode Island town which, like Newport, is on Narragansett Bay. In his design of that residence Charles McKim, who was to become the Gilded Age's greatest classical architect, anticipated many elements of modernism.

The exterior is composed of large, planar, unadorned surfaces; it derives its interest from its shape alone, rather than, as a classical structure would, from its shape and decoration both. (While this shape has often been repeated by the modernists, it is hardly functional: the roof serves as walls for the upper stories, and thereby much space is wasted.) The design is mainly asymmetrical, although there is a balance between some details, such as in the arrangement of the center group of window bays. The most frightening prediction of the house is the lack of decoration, even so much as the plaster panels of Ochre Point.

While it is true that much of the theory behind shingle style architecture anticipates modern theory, nevertheless the shingle style itself is not the modern. Traditionalists condemn the older style because they see what it helped bring about, and the modernists praise it for the same reason. If it can be seen without the prejudice of what came after, the shingle style proves to be very enjoyable. It had the sense to stay out of the city: it is an eccentric style, and the countryside and the resorts have a place for charming eccentricity.

Bristol, Rhode Island   *McKim, Mead and White, Architects*
SUMMER RESIDENCE OF WILLIAM LOW

Beacon Rock: Summer Residence of E. D. Morgan

Newport, Rhode Island

McKim, Mead and White, *Architects*

The predictions of the Low house were not to come true until a great age of architecture had crested and waned. McKim, Mead and White, who had produced that Bristol, Rhode Island, residence, produced in Newport a year later in 1888, Beacon Rock, a house that both heralded the new era of classicism and represented the types of designs for which that firm was to be best known. The patron in this case was E. D. Morgan, a financier; today the mansion is the summer home of Felix W. de Weldon.

In Beacon Rock, Ionic columns in rhythmic sets of six form colonnades about protruding wings and before a center section, the two gable roofs of which section cross the house and are connected by a widow's walk. The mansion of marble walls and tile roofs occupies one of the most dramatic sites in Newport. The modernist would feel—correctly—his style inequipped to build on a site of such natural beauty (made more beautiful by considerable blasting at the time of construction), and so he would try to design an unobtrusive house to "blend in" with its surroundings. The classicist has no such inconfidence, and realizes that, in the case of his style, nature plus the work of man can be more beautiful than nature alone. While the house does not attempt to appear something the tide washed up upon the shore, it nevertheless is perfectly suited to its site.

Newport, Rhode Island   *McKim, Mead and White, Architects*
BEACON ROCK: SUMMER RESIDENCE OF E. D. MORGAN

BEACON ROCK: SUMMER RESIDENCE OF E. D. MORGAN—AERIAL VIEW

BEACON ROCK: SUMMER RESIDENCE OF E. D. MORGAN—DINING ROOM

Marble House: Summer Residence of William Kissam Vanderbilt

Newport, Rhode Island

Richard Morris Hunt, *Architect*

In 1888, Mr. and Mrs. William Kissam Vanderbilt commissioned Richard Morris Hunt to design their Newport residence; the same patrons had hired that architect to design their famous New York City house (illustrated earlier herein), which had been such a turning point in the history of American architecture. Marble House, their Newport cottage, was opened on 19 August 1892, with nearly the same social fanfare as had ten years earlier greeted the housewarming of their New York mansion.

The exterior of Marble House is flawed in that it is too plain, and in that, like much of Hunt's other work, it appears top-heavy. The building ought to be wider from side to side; accordingly, the four Corinthian columns and their portico are too tall and thin. Although the exterior, particularly the ocean side, bears some sculptural decoration, there is not enough to relieve sufficiently the severity of the walls. Very helpful would have been statues standing upon the pedestals of the balustrade at the building's top. But these criticisms are minor, especially considering the improvement of classical buildings like Marble House over previous romantic structures.

The main entrance to the house is formed by a marvelous grill designed for the house by the architect and executed by John Williams Bronze Foundry of New York. Made of soft steel and gilt bronze, it weighs over ten tons. Before being moved to Marble House, the grill was publicly displayed in New York City to appropriately awed crowds. Through the door of the grill is reached the Marble House entrance hall, with its walls and floor of yellow Siena marble, and its beautiful staircase that has an Allard railing.

To the right of the entrance hall is the Gold Room, which acts as the ballroom. One of the most elaborate rooms in any Gilded Age cottage, gilt and marble are everywhere. The decoration is heavily derived from classical mythology: even the fireback shows Hades seizing Persephone.

Behind the ballroom is the Gothic room, meant to house a collection of medieval art objects, which has since been sold. On the opposite side of the building is the library, a rococo room with carved walnut shelves and decorated with an assortment of muses, cherubs, and clouds.

The dining room, which is in front of the library, is a very striking room. Its walls are of dark pink Numidian marble from Algeria. The Corinthian pilasters have gilt bronze bases and capitals. The chairs and stools use solid bronze frames, possibly the only such furniture in the world.

Newport, Rhode Island   *Richard Morris Hunt, Architect*
MARBLE HOUSE: SUMMER RESIDENCE OF WILLIAM KISSAM VANDERBILT

Marble House: Summer Residence of William Kissam Vanderbilt—
Great Hall

Marble House: Summer Residence of William Kissam Vanderbilt—
Gold Room

MARBLE HOUSE: SUMMER RESIDENCE OF WILLIAM KISSAM VANDERBILT—
DINING ROOM

Ascending the stairs, one finds on the mezzanine Mr. Vanderbilt's office to the left and Mrs. Vanderbilt's Louis XV sitting room to the right. From the second floor landing can be seen, on the back wall of the stair hall, medallions by Karl Bitter of, on the right, Jules Hardouin-Mansart, architect of Versailles, and, on the left, Richard Morris Hunt, architect of Marble House.

Mr. Vanderbilt's bedroom, which is in the restrained Louis XVI style, is behind the entrance portico. Mrs. Vanderbilt's bedroom, above the Gold Room, is in Louis XV, that elaborate style particularly noticeable here over the doors where cherubs hold shields bearing the letter A, for Alva, the first name of Mrs. Vanderbilt.

Behind Mrs. Vanderbilt's bedroom is that of her oldest son, William Kissam Vanderbilt, Jr. This room, which is more strictly American in its design, including the repeated eagle, than the cottage's other rooms, was evidently enlarged by the house's later owner, Frederick H. Prince, with space taken from the back bedroom that originally belonged to the Vanderbilt's daughter, Consuelo.

According to her mother's will, but certainly not her own, Consuelo in 1895 married the ninth Duke of Marlborough. The pair was divorced in 1920, and the next year Consuelo married Jacques Balsan. She died in 1965.

In 1896, Consuelo's mother, Alva, recently divorced from William Kissam Vanderbilt, married O. H. P. Belmont and closed Marble House, which

Vanderbilt had presented to her at the time of the cottage's housewarming. Mr. and Mrs. Belmont summered in Newport at Belcourt (shown later in this chapter) until his death in 1908, after which Alva reopened Marble House. There she continued to entertain regally, as well as to promote her cause of women's suffrage.

Above the Cliff Walk behind Marble House, she built the Chinese Teahouse in 1913; it was designed by Hunt and Hunt, the firm of the sons of Richard Morris Hunt. A little railroad from the mansion to the teahouse carried the servants bearing refreshments. Hopefully the teahouse, now in disrepair, will be restored in the future.

Mrs. Belmont never opened Marble House after the United States entered World War I. Just before her death in 1933, the house was sold for $100,000 to Frederick H. Prince, the Boston financier. When asked by a friend if he would not prefer a cozier home, Prince built a small but complete house, gardens included, on the roof of Marble House. He occupied the little house off and on for a time, but gradually lost interest, and decided in favor of the lower house. In 1963, Marble House was purchased from his trust by the Preservation Society of Newport County for $50,000, which was provided by Harold Stirling Vanderbilt, the youngest son of William Kissam and Alva. Today it is maintained in fine condition, although sparsely furnished; it is open to the public.

MARBLE HOUSE: SUMMER RESIDENCE OF WILLIAM KISSAM VANDERBILT—
MRS. VANDERBILT'S BEDROOM

Belcourt: Summer Residence of O. H. P. Belmont

Newport, Rhode Island

Richard Morris Hunt, *Architect*

Gilded Age aristocracy produced many rugged individualists (they could afford to be so); among them was Oliver Hazard Perry Belmont, whose granduncle was the naval hero and whose father was August Belmont, the Rothschilds' representative in the United States. Oliver Belmont's summer home, Belcourt, designed by Richard Morris Hunt and built between 1891 and 1894, is, as befitted its original owner, the most individualistic of all Newport mansions.

The house surrounds all four sides of an open court, beautiful indeed, in which exotic plants and animals were kept. Built in the style of a Louis XIII hunting lodge, Belcourt clearly shows the love Belmont had for horses. An American estate's stables were nearly always built as a structure separate from the main house, but almost the entire first floor of Belcourt was for use by horses. The low wing of the house contained stalls—of teakwood and English tiles—for 30 horses, and on the floor above were quarters for the grooms and other help. Guests could ride their horses or carriages right into the mansion, via a huge door at one end of the north wall of the high section of the house, and out an identical door on that wall's other end. Once inside, visitors would ride along a passageway the floor of which was pink marble inlay, and they could dismount to enter a vast hall whose floor space at the time was the largest of

Newport, Rhode Island   *Richard Morris Hunt, Architect*
BELCOURT: SUMMER RESIDENCE OF O. H. P. BELMONT

BELCOURT: SUMMER RESIDENCE OF O. H. P. BELMONT—SMALL DINING ROOM

BELCOURT: SUMMER RESIDENCE OF O. H. P. BELMONT—BALLROOM

that of any room in Newport; the hall was used for banquets and sometimes for carriage displays. This room's floor was in the same marble inlay as the carriage passageway floor; the process of fitting the thousands of chips for the two rooms took so much time that Belmont himself, to celebrate the completion of the work, laid the last chip, this one made of gold.

Pedestrians would enter by the formal doorway, which strangely was at the rear of the building. They, and those who rode into the house, would ascend a wooden staircase, copied from one at the Musée Cluny, and reach the elaborate apartment where Belmont resided. The staircase continued up to the third and highest story of the taller section of the building; the space on this floor was used for storage and so on. On the second floor, a hall, in carved oak and hung with red damask bearing the owner's initials, connects most rooms. The small dining room is exquisite with its oval-shaped, floor-length windows, and Adam ceiling. This opens on a beautiful parlor, where guests and host could retire after dinner. The Gothic ballroom has an upper row of stained-glass windows from thirteenth-century France, and a lower row made for the house. Opposite the upper windows, openings give way to the musicians' gallery. At one end of the ballroom is a small balcony for a few special guests, and at the other end a fireplace topped by a model of a castle. Although provision was made for 30 horses, there was no provision for human guests. Belmont's bedroom, decorated with painted scenes of medieval life, was the only bedroom in the house, except for those of the servants. Guests were put up at hotels, which Newport had, despite its snob appeal assertions to the contrary. Adjoining the bedroom, Belmont's bathroom had Scottish fixtures and the same English tiles used in the horse stalls.

In 1896, Belmont, previously a bachelor, married a rugged individualist—in fact, one of the ruggedest individualists of the Gilded Age. She was Alva Erskine Smith, who having just divorced William Kissam Vanderbilt in the first major society divorce, now owned two Bellevue Avenue estates, Belcourt, and Marble House. Belmont could not readily put her up at a hotel, and so converted a second-floor sitting room into her bedroom. A section to the south of the house was added for her son, Harold Stirling Vanderbilt, but was removed when he left the household.

Belmont died in 1908, and two years later Mrs. Belmont set about remodeling the house with the help of John Russell Pope. She replaced the three arches to the court with one, added French doors to the north wall of the court, converted some rooms into guest rooms, added an English library, and made other changes.

The house was sold out of the Belmont family in 1940, and passed through a number of hands until in 1956 it was acquired by Harold B. Tinney and his family. Noted artists and antique collectors, this talented family restored the house and furnished it with their collection. Like Mrs. Belmont, they altered the house; for example, they remodeled the second-floor loggia into a gallery of French furniture. They opened the major rooms to the public, while retaining a private section of the house for their own use. Despite the many alterations that have enriched Belcourt, it still remains the most masculine and personal of mansions, which is exactly what Oliver Belmont had in mind.

The Breakers: Summer Residence
of Cornelius Vanderbilt

Newport, Rhode Island

Richard Morris Hunt, *Architect*

The Breakers is probably the most famous of Gilded Age mansions and certainly one of the best. It was built for Cornelius Vanderbilt, head of the New York Central Railroad that his grandfather had founded. Cornelius II, in 1885, purchased for $4,000 an earlier home, also called The Breakers, from Pierre Lorillard when the tobacco tycoon left Newport for his new development, Tuxedo Park. The older Breakers was a shingle-style mansion built for Lorillard in 1878 to the designs of Peabody and Stearns. The house burned to the ground on 25 November 1892. Its replacement—designed to be fireproof—was finished in 1895. In it, Richard Morris Hunt pushed Gilded Age opulence to its limit, while never overstepping the bounds of good taste.

Still owned by the Vanderbilt family, The Breakers is open to the public under the auspices of the Preservation Society of Newport County. The kitchen and pantry areas, of interest in their own right, are on display, not often the case among Gilded Age mansions that can be toured. Even rarer, the house still has its original furnishings.

Italian Renaissance is the style of the five-story cottage. The front facing the land is far more austere than the sea front, which presents shade and light, loggias and terraces, columns and sculpture.

The interiors do not include a ballroom as such; the monumental Great Hall serves the purpose. The dining room is certainly one of the country's most elaborate interiors, a tribute to the Baroque. The dazzling morning and music rooms were built in France for the cottage, knocked down, and reassembled in Newport. Probably the most unique interior is the billiard room, which consists mainly of alabaster and marble.

The grounds at the Breakers are tiny, considering the size of the mansion. A children's playhouse by Peabody and Stearns was added to the estate while Vanderbilt still occupied the earlier house. When Hunt rebuilt The Breakers, he did not want the stables to crowd the small plot, so built them a few blocks away, at Coggeshall and Bateman Avenues. These, too, are open to the public through the Preservation Society, and contain a fine collection of Gilded Age carriages and tack.

THE BREAKERS: SUMMER RESIDENCE OF CORNELIUS VANDERBILT—A GATE

Newport, Rhode Island   *Richard Morris Hunt, Architect*
THE BREAKERS: SUMMER RESIDENCE OF CORNELIUS VANDERBILT

THE BREAKERS: SUMMER RESIDENCE OF CORNELIUS VANDERBILT—GREAT HALL

The Breakers: Summer Residence of Cornelius Vanderbilt—Dining Room

Georgian Court: Summer Residence of George J. Gould

Lakewood, New Jersey

Bruce Price, *Architect*

According to Bruce Price, its architect, Georgian Court is "an attempt to put a French chateau roof on an English Georgian house." Such willingness to pick and choose earned for the main body of Gilded Age architecture the accurate title "eclecticism." The name does not imply a haphazard amalgam of elements: the house and the roof of Georgian Court combine perfectly. And they combine to produce what could only be an American building, an identity the thoroughly New Jersey setting of lake and pines emphasizes. American eclectic architecture is like American civilization: elements from the world over are joined together to form a result unmistakably American.

The interior of the mansion is very lavish, while remaining light enough to suit the house's resort location. In the great hall, the splendid bronze railing of the staircase continues across the balcony; facing the balcony is a frieze, painted by Robert Sewall, of scenes from the Canterbury Tales. The fine conservatory is roofed and walled in glass. The music room is elaborately paneled, and the painting of the library ceiling is exceptional.

The mansion was built in 1897-1899 for George J. Gould, son of Jay Gould, the despised financier. Currently it is the seat of Georgian Court College, a Catholic school for women. The house still holds many of its original furnishings, and is scrupulously maintained, as are the extraordinary grounds that contain such features as a marble gondola launch, a vast electric fountain, and an enormous stable, which cleverly incorporates the estate's water tower. With the exception of some new buildings added by the college, the estate remains almost exactly as it was when occupied by the Goulds.

Lakewood, New Jersey   *Bruce Price, Architect*
GEORGIAN COURT: SUMMER RESIDENCE OF GEORGE J. GOULD

Georgian Court: Summer Residence of George J. Gould—Great Hall

Georgian Court: Summer Residence of George J. Gould—Dining Room

Georgian Court: Summer Residence of George J. Gould—Drawing Room

GEORGIAN COURT: SUMMER RESIDENCE OF GEORGE J. GOULD—CONSERVATORY

GEORGIAN COURT: SUMMER RESIDENCE OF GEORGE J. GOULD—MUSIC ROOM

GEORGIAN COURT: SUMMER RESIDENCE OF GEORGE J. GOULD—LIBRARY

GEORGIAN COURT: SUMMER RESIDENCE OF GEORGE J. GOULD—STABLE

High Tide: Summer Residence of William Starr Miller

Newport, Rhode Island

Whitney Warren, *Architect*

Soon after Bellevue Avenue becomes the Ocean Drive, High Tide appears suddenly, as if by magic. That force might account for the conflicting impressions given by the house. It looks small, but a closer look reveals it is actually extensive. It looks rambling, but there is definite order to its shape. With its flowing roof it looks rustic, but its sophisticated fenestration does not. The house appears to be simplicity itself, but it is filled with Beaux Arts interiors.

High Tide has a magical site. From a high hill, the house overlooks Bailey's Beach, always Newport's most exclusive watering hole, and, beyond that, the Atlantic Ocean. The tangled foliage around Almy's Pond at one side of the house supplies a nature setting, while on the estate's other side is a more civilized scene including Crossways, by architect Dudley Newton, the 1898 giant colonial-style summer residence of Stuyvesant Fish and his legendary wife, Mame Fish. High Tide, built in 1900, was designed by Whitney Warren for his sister and her husband William Starr Miller. It is currently owned by Hickman Price, Jr.

Newport, Rhode Island   *Whitney Warren, Architect*
HIGH TIDE: SUMMER RESIDENCE OF WILLIAM STARR MILLER

Rosecliff: Summer Residence of Hermann Oelrichs

Newport, Rhode Island

McKim, Mead and White, *Architects*

George Bancroft, the historian who founded the United States Naval Academy at Annapolis, built the first Rosecliff, naming it after the product which, along with artichokes, he particularly fostered in his gardening on the cottage's Newport site between the Cliff Walk and Bellevue Avenue. After Bancroft's death in 1891, the estate was purchased by Hermann Oelrichs, agent of the North German Lloyd steamship line, and his wife, the greater source of the pair's wealth, the former Theresa Fair, whose father James Graham Fair literally struck it rich with the Comstock Lode at Virginia City, Nevada, history's richest vein of silver and gold.

In 1900, the original Rosecliff and most of its gardens disappeared to make way for the present mansion by Stanford White, of McKim, Mead and White. White fashioned from white terra-cotta a sumptuous exterior, rich in decoration such as the spandrel swags above the first-floor doors, and such as the Vitruvian scroll linking the second-story windows. The sculptures on the building, as well as on the grounds, are by Augustus St. Gaudens. The house has an underground basement that contains the kitchen, chauffeur's apartment, wine cellar, and the like. A third story contains the servants' sleeping quarters and is inobstrusively plain and recessed behind the roof balustrade.

The ballroom is Newport's largest, 40 by 60 feet, but even its size is not as important as its delicate plasterwork. Among other first-floor rooms are the billiard room, the salon with its grand fireplace, and the dining room. A white, heart-shaped, marble stair-

Newport, Rhode Island   *McKim, Mead and White, Architects*
ROSECLIFF: SUMMER RESIDENCE OF HERMANN OELRICHS

ROSECLIFF: SUMMER RESIDENCE OF HERMANN OELRICHS—BALLROOM

case leads to nine second-floor bedrooms.

Rosecliff on 19 August 1904 was the scene of the famous Bal Blanc, at which all the women wore white dresses and powdered hair or white wigs, the men wore black-and-white evening dress, and even a floodlit fleet of white boats was anchored off the Cliff Walk.

Hermann Oelrichs died in 1906, Tessie in 1926. Their only son, Hermann, sold the cottage in 1941 to a real estate dealer. For $21,000, not at all untypical of prices during the 1940s for Newport mansions, which Henry James had once called "white elephants," the house came to be the property of Gertrude Niesen, the torch singer. She left the estate unguarded during winter; the oil burner failed; the pipes froze and burst. An ice-filled house and a water bill of over $800 convinced Miss Niesen to sell the mansion to Ray Alan Van Clief, who, in the late 1940s sold it in turn to J. Edgar Monroe. He and his family restored and refurnished the house, and spent their summers there until 1971 when he gave the house and an endowment to the Preservation Society of Newport County, which since 1972 has opened it to the public.

ROSECLIFF: SUMMER RESIDENCE OF HERMANN OELRICHS—DINING ROOM

ROSECLIFF: SUMMER RESIDENCE OF HERMANN OELRICHS—STAIRCASE

Vernon Court: Summer Residence of Richard Gambrill

Newport, Rhode Island

Carrere and Hastings, *Architects*

Like many buildings by Carrere and Hastings, Vernon Court derives great power from its verticality. Since the windows are sunken in the walls and the size of the cornice is reduced, there is little to keep the eye from rising; the many tall, identical chimneys continue the ascent even beyond the high, pitched roof. Still, this is a resort cottage, and the necessary softening is provided by the two loggias, one at each end of the main section of the structure. Unlike the main section, the loggias are horizontal and highly decorated, including the playful sculpture groups at each roof corner.

The interior of the main section is again powerful and formal, while the frieze and ceiling of the loggias were painted by James Wall Finn to show vases with flowers and birds under a trellised arbor.

The cottage was built in 1900-1901 for Richard Gambrill. The garden by Wadley and Smythe is a recreation of Henry VIII's for Anne Boleyn at Hampton Court. Until recently, the Newport estate was occupied by Vernon Court Junior College, an institution for women; the college has been disbanded, and the future of the mansion is in doubt.

Newport, Rhode Island   *Carrere and Hastings, Architects*
VERNON COURT: SUMMER RESIDENCE OF RICHARD GAMBRILL

VERNON COURT: SUMMER RESIDENCE OF RICHARD GAMBRILL—SMALL SALON

VERNON COURT: SUMMER RESIDENCE OF RICHARD GAMBRILL—LOGGIA

The Elms: Summer Residence of Edward Julius Berwind

Newport, Rhode Island

Horace Trumbauer, *Architect*

The Gilded Age was fascinated and somewhat awed by the civilizations of Europe, and so adapted to American soil not only a number of European architectural styles, but sometimes the designs of individual structures as well. The modeling of an American building upon a European one upsets the modernists no end, with their emphasis on originality and home-grown edifices. But the practice of close-copying worked so well—in other words, it produced works of such beauty—that it seems a hard practice for a practical person to condemn.

All classical architects of the Gilded Age copied foreign buildings at some time, but none was more insistent on doing so than Horace Trumbauer. For The Elms, the summer residence of Edward Julius Berwind, Trumbauer chose as a model the Chateau d'Argenson at Asnières. That chateau is a product of eighteenth-century France, whose style Trumbauer, at home in all styles, particularly called his own. And, galling to purists Trumbauer in The Elms, as he did in most all his designs, improved upon his model.

Newport, Rhode Island   *Horace Trumbauer, Architect*
THE ELMS: SUMMER RESIDENCE OF EDWARD JULIUS BERWIND

THE ELMS: SUMMER RESIDENCE OF EDWARD JULIUS BERWIND—STAIRCASE

His patron, Edward Julius Berwind, was originally a Philadelphian, but lived most of his adult life in New York; in 1894 he built an Italian mansion at Sixty-fourth Street and Fifth Avenue in that city. His fortune came mainly from coal, a heat and energy source of special importance during the Gilded Age. Berwind in 1888 bought a Newport home, The Elms; it stood on the site of the present mansion, which replaced the original cottage in 1899-1902.

The entrance facade is hard by Bellevue Avenue and separated from that street by a high fence with urns and lanterns. The facade consists of an elaborate center section and relatively plain wings. Four Corinthian columns surround and divide three arched doorways, each filled by wrought-iron gates. A second-floor balustrade carries an urn above each first-story column, and a rectangular window on the second story corresponds to each arch below. As the utility rooms are concealed in the basement, so the servants' quarters, which make up the third floor, are concealed behind a parapet wall that surrounds the top of the house. Upon this wall rest four sculpture groups that alleviate an otherwise straight roofline. The wing's windows have segmental arches on the first floor, and are rectangular on the second; this pattern continues on the sides and the garden front's wings. The center section of the garden front presses outward with curved sides. Doors and windows are in segmental arches, and there is a profusion of sculpture, even in the pediment.

Inside the front door of the entrance facade is a vast and varied interior space. This is divided between the foyer, the hall, and the staircase, and even, by way of the hall, into the ballroom. The foyer's white marble floor with green border leads to steps rising between two Ionic columns with Breccia marble shafts and gilt bronze bases and capitals. At the first floor, the staircase divides in halves to be joined again at a landing and continue in a single flight to the second floor hall. The staircase has white marble stairs and a wrought-iron and bronze railing. Limestone walls surround the stairwell. Throughout the space made by these different interior areas is architectural decoration, such as the hall ceiling designs, which greatly enhance and enrich the space.

The ballroom is 41 by 49 feet, and rises to 19 feet, 3 inches. It is a light room for all its size; even its corners are curved to add to the flow of its lines. To the north of the ballroom are a Venetian dining room and a Chinoiserie breakfast room; to its south a Louis XVI drawing room and an especially airy conservatory. Other first-story rooms are a majestic library, juxtaposed in location and atmosphere to the conservatory, and a pair of alcoves, one on either side of the stairwell.

The ornate second-floor hall, which includes Breccia pilasters, opens on a number of bedrooms, both

THE ELMS: SUMMER RESIDENCE OF EDWARD JULIUS BERWIND—CONSERVATORY

those for guests and those for Mr. and Mrs. Berwind. Although all are splendidly decorated, they are relatively small: a Newport holiday is not to be spent in one's bedroom. A second-floor living room, above the ballroom, overlooks the park.

The more organized grounds around an estate are called a park. The park of The Elms is one of the largest and most splendid in Newport. It was designed by Trumbauer himself, although Charles H. Miller and Ernest W. Bowditch aided in selection of planting, as the estate's long-time gardener Bruce Butterton probably did also. The park's beauty depends not only on nature, which itself is clipped and refined by man, but also on an array of sculpture and architectural features.

Adjoining the park to the north, a terrace holds the glorious carriage house and garage. These buildings, which match each other, were built in 1909-1911 to Trumbauer's designs.

The house passed out of the Berwind family's possession at the death of its last occupant, Edward Julius Berwind's sister, Julia Berwind, who died in 1961, aged 91 years. The syndicate that purchased the estate from the family were planning to demolish the mansion and develop the land, but the property was purchased in 1962 by the Preservation Society of Newport County, which opened it to the public.

Whitehall: Winter Residence of Henry Morrison Flagler

Palm Beach, Florida

Carrere and Hastings, *Architects*

More wonderful than any palace in Europe, grander and more magnificent than any other private dwelling in the world is Whitehall, the new home Henry M. Flagler has built in the land of flowers for his bride. . . . Mrs. Flagler can bid her friends welcome to a home which in point of grandeur queen or princess never knew.

—New York Herald, 30 March 1902

W ell, not quite. But these lines of Gilded Age newspaper reporting do show the confidence of the period, and certainly Whitehall is among the world's most magnificent dwellings. Henry Morrison Flagler, who (as can be seen in the chapter on hotels) played an important part in the development of Florida, erected Whitehall in 1901-1902 for his third wife, the former Mary Lily Kenan. She had told him she had always dreamed of living in marble halls. Flagler, eager to comply, ordered plans from Carrere and Hastings for a Cuban-style villa. The designs evolved into a more American house, but still retained was the Spanish concept of a central court.

Immediately behind the Doric entrance portico is an authentic Marble Hall, 110 feet long, 40 feet wide, 20 feet high. The ceiling bears medallions depicting Air, Earth, Fire, and Water, and has at its

Palm Beach, Florida　　　　　　　　*Carrere and Hastings, Architects*
WHITEHALL: WINTER RESIDENCE OF HENRY MORRISON FLAGLER

center a dome in which is painted *The Crowning of Knowledge*.

The Louis XIV music room doubles as an art gallery. Interrupting the walls covered with paintings is a very large organ, a seemingly indispensable fixture for a big Gilded Age mansion. In this room again, the ceiling has a central dome, this one containing a depiction of Aurora.

The ceiling of the François I dining room is divided into panels, each decorated with papier-mâché of green and gold, colors repeated throughout the room. Other first-story rooms are the Swiss billiard room, with its Caen stone fireplace; the Italian Renaissance library; the Louis XVI salon; the Elizabethan breakfast room; and the mirrored, white-and-gold Louis XV ballroom. The floor also contains a suite of offices for Flagler and his staff.

The white marble staircase rises to the bedrooms, decorated in many styles. The bedrooms include not only those meant for Mr. and Mrs. Flagler, but also sixteen guest rooms, an indication of the extensive entertaining Mrs. Flagler greatly enjoyed, and Mr. Flagler, for her sake, obligingly withstood.

Mr. Flagler's death came in 1913, Mrs. Flagler's in 1917. In 1925, their heirs sold Whitehall, and, with the addition of a 12-story, 300-room building, it became a hotel. Whitehall Hotel went out of business in 1959, and the house was purchased by Mrs. Flagler Matthews, granddaughter of H. M. Flagler. Since February of the following year, it has been open as the Henry Morrison Flagler Museum.

WHITEHALL: WINTER RESIDENCE OF HENRY MORRISON FLAGLER—MARBLE HALL

WHITEHALL: WINTER RESIDENCE OF HENRY MORRISON FLAGLER—MUSIC ROOM

WHITEHALL: WINTER RESIDENCE OF HENRY MORRISON FLAGLER—DINING ROOM

Miramar: Summer Residence
of Mrs. George D. Widener

Newport. Rhode Island

Horace Trumbauer, *Architect*

Miramar is light as a cloud. The big building appears to be weightless, especially on a sun-filled, heady day at Newport, a city which is itself one of the Gilded Age's greatest illusions. The cottage's lightness is due to the skill of its architect, Horace Trumbauer, and was enhanced by the fanciful gardens of Jacques Greber. The pair also collaborated on Lynnewood, the spectacular estate of P. A. B. Widener in Elkins Park, Pennsylvania, which house (illustrated in the previous chapter) was occupied also by P. A. B.'s son, George, who began Miramar. George Widener went down with the *Titanic* along with his son, Harry Elkins Widener, for whom the huge Harvard library, also by Trumbauer, was named. His widow lived in the finished Newport cottage, as did her new husband, Dr. Alexander Hamilton Rice, the explorer.

The house sits well shielded from Bellevue Avenue by foliage; along the road runs an iron fence bearing the Widener initial, which looks like a Sèvres mark

turned sideways. The rear of the building overlooks the Cliff Walk. The grounds contain figures and fountains as well as a beautiful garage. The house itself has a rusticated first story with arched windows and doors. The rectangular windows of the second story are separated from each other by plaques bearing music instruments or other decoration. The roof, which comprises the third story where the servants' quarters are located, is recessed behind the balustrade that surrounds the house.

The interior, as befits the outside and the very idea of a summer cottage, is also usually light and airy, although sometimes it becomes somewhat sombre for a change of mood. Among the gay rooms are the salon, with the exterior plaques reflected in the room's upper panels; the marble dining room, breathtaking with its extraordinary wall hanging; and the breakfast room, bright and cheerful while elegant, and with a marble floor in a geometric design.

The house served for a time as a private school for girls, and has recently changed hands again. Miramar's gardens have long since lost their original order, and the iron fence is rotting away. One of the most beautiful of all Newport's cottages, the maintenance of the house and the restoration of the grounds is to be very much desired.

Newport, Rhode Island   *Horace Trumbauer, Architect*
MIRAMAR: SUMMER RESIDENCE OF MRS. GEORGE D. WIDENER

MIRAMAR: SUMMER RESIDENCE OF MRS. GEORGE D. WIDENER—SALON

MIRAMAR: SUMMER RESIDENCE OF MRS. GEORGE D. WIDENER—DINING ROOM

MIRAMAR: SUMMER RESIDENCE OF MRS. GEORGE D. WIDENER—BREAKFAST ROOM

Vizcaya: Winter Residence of James Deering

Miami, Florida

F. Burrall Hoffman, Jr., *Architect*

A handsome Italian villa in its own right, Vizcaya is enhanced by its magnificent furnishings and its gardens, generally considered the finest classical gardens in America. F. Burrall Hoffman, Jr., was the architect for the 1914-1916 house, as well as for the many other splendid smaller buildings on the grounds. Diego Suarez designed the gardens. Paul Chalfin was artistic supervisor for all aspects of the estate.

The house consists of four pavilions linked by long sections that surround a central courtyard. The exterior of the structure derives from several Italian buildings from the sixteenth and seventeenth cen-turies. Vizcaya contains an unusually large number of rooms for a resort cottage. This allows the interior styles to reflect a wide range of Italian cities and periods, and to include such rooms as the Adam library and Biedermeier guest room, which derive from other cultures. The number of rooms also reduces the size of each, giving every interior its own unity and compact intricacy.

The house looks directly out on Biscayne Bay and on a breakwater that Alexander Stirling Calder carved from native coral rock.

The original owner was James Deering, cofounder of International Harvester. A bachelor, he spent his winters at Vizcaya from 1916 to his death in 1925, when he left the house to his heirs. Since 1952, it has been open to the public under the auspices of Dade County.

Miami, Florida   *F. Burrall Hoffman, Jr., Architect*
VIZCAYA: WINTER RESIDENCE OF JAMES DEERING
At the front of the picture is the breakwater.

VIZCAYA: WINTER RESIDENCE OF JAMES DEERING—RECEPTION ROOM

VIZCAYA: WINTER RESIDENCE OF JAMES DEERING—RENAISSANCE HALL

VIZCAYA: WINTER RESIDENCE OF JAMES DEERING—GARDEN

5
Hotels

With a smaller percentage of the population than today traveling far from home during the Gilded Age, hotels not only were stopping places for out-of-town visitors, but also were, more often than now, service apartments for regular tenants. Comfort on a par with that the traveler enjoyed at home was not always available to him in hotels, as it generally is at present; for instance, the private bathroom was rare. The run-of-the-mill hotel of the Gilded Age was an improvement over the often dismal rooms of the inns of previous eras, but nevertheless not the usually welcome change of pace that hotels are now.

But that was hotels in general. The luxury hotels of the Gilded Age were far better than those being built today. The suites of the older hotels had to please even visitors from posh country estates; the ballrooms, restaurants, and other common rooms of those hotels provided a glittering setting for social life. Fortunately, such elegance is still to be found today in many of the many hotels that remain from that past era.

The Ponce de Leon

St. Augustine, Florida

Carrere and Hastings, *Architects*

St. Augustine is the oldest city in the United States. Another reason for its importance is the fascination it held for Henry Morrison Flagler, who played a tremendous part in shaping Florida's development. Flagler (whose Florida residence is described earlier in these pages) first visited the state in 1878 with his wife, who was seeking health. His attraction to Florida, and particularly to St. Augustine, led him to begin constructing at that city in 1885 the first of his several hotels in that state. Carrere and Hastings were the architects. On the last day of 1885, Flagler purchased the Jacksonville, St. Augustine and Halifax River Railroad, which was to become in the future part of the Florida East Coast line, the railroad that opened eastern Florida. The hotel opened on 10 January 1888; Flagler, the latter-day discoverer of Florida, had appropriately named the hotel the Ponce de Leon after the state's original discoverer.

Between the front ends of the two ells that extend forward from the center section of this Spanish Rennaissance hotel is a screen with an imposing gate. The resulting courtyard is 150 feet square and has a magnificent fountain at its center. The two towers, one each on the east and west wings, rise to 165 feet.

The main walls of the Ponce de Leon are of poured concrete, one of the first examples of this type of construction in America.

The hotel's common rooms are rich in decoration. The rotunda serves as the hotel lobby; between the elaborate mosaic floor and the vast dome are numerous columns, including oak caryatids, and life-size wall paintings of Adventure, Discovery, Conquest, and Civilization. The ballroom has a large onyx mantel, and the ceilings in that room, as well as in the parlor and drawing room, are painted with cupids and garlands by Virgilio Tojetti. In the oval salon, oak columns support a vast dome, and the decorations include Spanish galleys, coats of arms of Spanish provinces, and, by George W. Maynard, an epitomized history of Florida on silver panels. The hotel had 450 private rooms and suites, all lavishly furnished.

For travelers of more modest means, Flagler erected a second hotel, the Alcazar, which stood across the street from the Ponce de Leon. The Alcazar was designed by Carrere and Hastings, as was the Ponce de Leon, and was in the Spanish Renaissance style of the larger hotel, but with Moorish touches. Built in 1887-1888, the smaller building held 75 private rooms. It now houses city government offices and a museum.

In 1967, the Ponce de Leon became Flagler College, a school for women. It remains carefully preserved, important history in an historical city.

THE PONCE DE LEON—THE ROTUNDA

Elkins Park, Pennsylvania   *Horace Trumbauer, Architect*
RESIDENCE OF GEORGE W. ELKINS

Cambridge, Massachusetts   *Welles Bosworth, Architect*
GRAND COURT, MASSACHUSETTS INSTITUTE OF TECHNOLOGY

Newport, Rhode Island   *McKim, Mead and White, Architects*
ROSECLIFF: SUMMER RESIDENCE OF HERMANN OELRICHS

St. Augustine, Florida   *Carrere and Hastings, Architects*
THE PONCE DE LEON
The hotel is seen here as it nears completion.

THE PONCE DE LEON—SIDE PARLOR OFF BALLROOM

THE PONCE DE LEON—DINING ROOM

Elkins Park, Pennsylvania　　　　　　　　　　　*Horace Trumbauer, Architect*
RESIDENCE OF GEORGE W. ELKINS

Cambridge, Massachusetts   *Welles Bosworth, Architect*
GRAND COURT, MASSACHUSETTS INSTITUTE OF TECHNOLOGY

Newport, Rhode Island   *McKim, Mead and White, Architects*
ROSECLIFF: SUMMER RESIDENCE OF HERMANN OELRICHS

St. Augustine, Florida   *Carrere and Hastings, Architects*
THE PONCE DE LEON
The hotel is seen here as it nears completion.

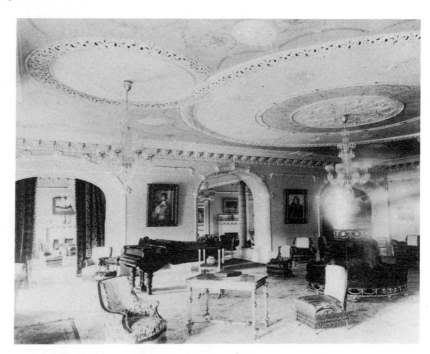

THE PONCE DE LEON—SIDE PARLOR OFF BALLROOM

THE PONCE DE LEON—DINING ROOM

THE PONCE DE LEON—THE ROTUNDA

The Brown Palace

Denver, Colorado

Frank E. Edbrooke, *Architect*

The origins of the Brown Palace Hotel combine influences from the East, the Midwest, and most importantly the West. Denver found its aristocracy in the men that found their wealth in the mines and railroads of the West. For Easterners who had traveled to Denver to confer with the city's millionaires, Henry C. Brown decided in 1888 to build a palatial hotel, for the design of which he was to hire a Midwesterner, Chicagoan Frank E. Edbrooke.

The hotel, which was shaped to fit a triangular plot of ground left over from some land Brown had purchased in 1863 for development, had its design likewise touched by the East, Midwest, and West. The desire to please cosmopolitan Easterners resulted in the structure's style being Italian Renaissance. But Edbrooke was too much a part of the Chicago school for the building not to bear the mark of such Chicago structures as Richardson's 1887 Marshall Field Warehouse and Adler and Sullivan's 1889 Auditorium Building. The West manifested itself in the Denver edifice in many ways, most noticeably in the bravura that penetrated the structure and its atmosphere. The nature that abounded in the West is referred to in James Whitehouse's series of 26 medallions on the seventh-floor spandrels, each medallion carved to show a different animal, although not necessarily an animal native to the West. Western materials that hung on the steel and wrought-iron frame included Colorado red granite and brown Arizona sandstone.

Each guest room faces on a street, and is reached via one of the balconies, which, with their beautiful grill railings, surround the lobby. The hotel's largest interior, the lobby rises through the first seven floors. The main dining room looks out on views of the Rocky Mountains from the eighth floor; other public areas throughout the hotel included the Turkish baths, hairdressing parlors and barber shops, billiard rooms, a bowling alley, a library, and a beautiful salon called the Onyx Room.

Today, as at its formal opening on 28 January 1893, the Brown Palace takes pride in being an up-to-date hotel; accordingly, many interiors have been changed, although the lobby basically remains a fine period piece. In 1959, the hotel opened a modern 22-floor addition, which is joined to the old building across Tremont Street and does not interfere with the architecture of the original structure. The architectural firm of William B. Tabler designed the addition. No matter the newness of the addition, the lover of the Old West will have more fun staying in the old building.

Denver, Colorado   *Frank E. Edbrooke, Architect*

THE BROWN PALACE

Typical Bedroom

Typical Bathroom

The Brown Palace—Lobby

The Waldorf-Astoria

New York, New York

Henry J. Hardenbergh, *Architect*

William Waldorf Astor decided his wife, born Mary Paul, should be the reigning Mrs. Astor, replacing Caroline Schermerhorn Astor in that role. When society as a whole, Caroline Schermerhorn Astor, and even Mary Paul Astor showed no interest in making the switch, Astor moved in a huff to England, where he and his wife founded the British branch of the family. As revenge on Caroline Astor, he left instructions that his New York City residence, which stood at Fifth Avenue and Thirty-third Street next to the famous 350 Fifth Avenue brownstone in which the definite Mrs. Astor held court, be demolished and a dazzling hotel be built in its place. He called the hotel the Waldorf, in honor of his mother's family.

The Waldorf, designed by Henry J. Hardenbergh, was a 13-story building, supposedly German Renaissance, but actually close to the romantic tradition. Its owner was George Boldt, who later built the Bellevue-Stratford in Philadelphia. Boldt was assisted in running the New York hotel by Oscar Tschirky, who became known as Oscar of the Waldorf. Among the hotel's most elaborate interiors were the Palm Garden, the Empire Room, and Peacock Alley, the corridor that gained its name for the nightly parade of society.

In 1895, soon after the opening of the Waldorf, Caroline Astor, her exclusivity threatened, fled to the new mansion at Sixty-fifth Street and Fifth Avenue that, soon after construction was begun on the Waldorf, Richard Morris Hunt had been commissioned to design. (The new mansion is shown elsewhere in this book.) The brownstone came tumbling down, and in its place arose another Boldt hotel. This one was backed by Caroline Astor's side of the family,

New York, New York   *Henry J. Hardenbergh, Architect*

THE WALDORF-ASTORIA

The completed hotel, seen from the Thirty-fourth Street side which agreed to have it run conjointly with the Waldorf, provided that the newer structure was built technically separate from the older, and that provision was made so that the newer hotel could be bricked off from the older, in the event the feud reheated.

The rivalry had caused John Jacob Astor, Caroline Astor's son, to have Hardenbergh design a hotel taller than the Waldorf by five stories, and more elaborate, both inside and out, including a posher Peacock Alley. The older hotel had opened on 13 March 1893; the newer opened on 1 November 1895. John Jacob Astor had wanted to follow William Waldorf Astor's lead by naming the new hotel after his mother's family. The combined hotel, which held 1,000 guest rooms and suites, three-quarters of which had private baths, was barely saved from being called the Waldorf-Schermerhorn through a suggestion to instead name the new section the Astoria.

Both structures were demolished in autumn of 1929 and replaced by the present Waldorf-Astoria, a single building designed by Schultze and Weaver; that hotel opened in October 1931 and is located at Park Avenue and Forty-ninth Street. On the site of the old Waldorf-Astoria, the Empire State Building was built during the 1930s.

THE WALDORF-ASTORIA—THIRTY-THIRD STREET ENTRANCE
Seen in 1893, this was the main entrance to the Waldorf Hotel

THE WALDORF—MEN'S CAFE

THE ASTORIA—FOUR-SIDED MAHOGANY BAR

THE WALDORF-ASTORIA—THE SECOND PEACOCK ALLEY

The Royal Poinciana

Palm Beach, Florida

McQuire and McDonald, *Builders*

His Ponce de Leon Hotel a success, Henry Morrison Flagler continued his creation of an "American Riviera," extending his railroad and planting his hotels further and further down the east coast of Florida. When he reached Palm Beach, he created what has been from its inception to the present the most socially prominent winter resort in America. He began laying out the community in 1893, and 1 May of the same year saw the start of construction there of his largest hotel, the Royal Poinciana, presumably from the designs of its builders, McQuire and McDonald. On 11 February of the next year, the hotel opened and proved such a success that it had to be expanded in 1889 and 1901, until the total number of guest rooms was about 1,200. Train service reached West Palm Beach on 2 April 1894, and private cars were soon regularly making their way over the trestle Flagler had built between the sandspit and the mainland.

The Royal Poinciana as first built, and the hotel with its additions, bears the shape of the letter F, which many thought stood for Florida, while some knew better. The main entrance was a portico extending from between its colonnade wings; above was a well-proportioned tower. The public rooms, such as the rotunda and dining room, were elegant, although not as elaborate as the Ponce de Leon's counterparts.

Flagler was to go on with his settling of Florida. He eventually built a bridge across the Florida Keys; the first two trains arrived 22 January 1912, bearing the 82-year-old tycoon and his guests. The Key West roadbed was washed away during a hurricane in 1935, the year after the Royal Poinciana was demolished due to hurricane damage.

Palm Beach, Florida   *McQuire and McDonald, Builders*

THE ROYAL POINCIANA

The Royal Poinciana—Rotunda

The Royal Poinciana—Dining Room

Sherry's Hotel
New York, New York
McKim, Mead and White, *Architects*

During the Gilded Age, as today, restaurants were often housed in one part of large buildings, rather than occupying an entire smaller structure. Hotels were many times the homes of restaurants, and sometimes the restaurant possessed a fame and identity almost independent of the hotel. Such was the case with the famous restaurant Louis Sherry maintained on the first floor of the 1898 Sherry's Hotel at Fifth Avenue and Forty-fourth Street in New York City, a structure by McKim, Mead and White.

The two-story Ionic piers that surrounded the base of the hotel's exterior set off the restaurant and cafe, which was also on the first floor, from upper stories. Inside the restaurant, Roman Ionic piers of oak and gold supported the ceiling that was hung with crystal chandeliers. The atmosphere of starched white linen made for unsurpassed elegance in dining.

The third floor of the hotel contained the ballroom, extravagant in its interior, and like the restaurant, specially set off on the exterior. Seven floors of well-appointed rooms rose above the ballroom level.

Diagonally across the street was another famous contemporary restaurant, Delmonico's. Between the two restaurants, both of which were in buildings now demolished, were shared a large number of tales of upper-class life during the Gilded Age.

New York, New York   *McKim, Mead and White, Architects*
SHERRY'S HOTEL

Sherry's Hotel—Dining Room

The Ansonia

New York, New York

Graves and Duboy, *Architects*

New York City's West Side retains (only temporarily, it is feared) a number of the fabulous hotel-apartment combinations that the Gilded Age excelled in designing. Among those on the West Side are the three As—the Alwyn, the Althorp, and the Ansonia. The third is especially famous for its connections with the city's musical life, from the occupancy of the music teachers that generations of New York children have trudged off to see to the habitation by the Great Ziegfeld, who by his nature must have been impressed not only with the musicality of the structure's design, but also with its theatricality.

The 17-story Ansonia was built in 1900 from the plans of Graves and Duboy, who were employed by W. E. D. Stokes. Its French design cannot be quickly described, but to remark the building is a beautiful collection of all sorts of architectural elements and details, all sumptuously shaped, and crowned by mansard roofs.

New York, New York   *Graves and Duboy, Architects*

THE ANSONIA

The Bellevue-Stratford

Philadelphia, Pennsylvania

G. W. and W. D. Hewitt, *Architects*

At midnight, 19 September 1901, the old Bellevue Hotel on the northwest corner of Broad and Walnut Streets in Philadelphia closed. The guests went across the street to the southwest corner, the former site of the Stratford Hotel, where the new Bellevue-Stratford Hotel opened at one minute past midnight. The architects were the Hewitt Brothers and the owner George C. Boldt, the immigrant who had risen from waiter to the owner of two great hyphenated hotels, the other being the Waldorf-Astoria.

The first two stories form a rusticated base, upon which rests a high section of rusticated walls with bays. Above the bays, balconies introduce a section with walls not rusticated but with a profusion of decoration growing more and more ornate as the lavishly decorated mansard roof is approached. Within the hotel decoration is also very rich, especially in the ballroom, which the Kniesel Quintette opened less than two months after the hotel's opening, and which was immortalized by the annual Assembly Ball.

Philadelphia, Pennsylvania   *G. W. and W. D. Hewitt, Architects*
THE BELLEVUE-STRATFORD

The Copley Plaza

Boston, Massachusetts

Henry J. Hardenbergh, *Architect*

Henry J. Hardenbergh designed hotels that come to the minds of many people when the splendor of Gilded Age luxury hotels is mentioned. The Willard Hotel, built in Washington in 1901, recently closed its doors, but New York's current Plaza, erected in 1907, is still the center of the city's social life. The Copley Plaza in Boston dates from 1912, a year the elegance of which it continues to reflect.

The main facade of the building faces Copley Square (an adjacent side of which is occupied by the Boston Public Library, a building illustrated later in this book). The rusticated surface of the seven-story facade bears three stringcourses, and is crowned by a cornice and balustrade. The oval shape of the main dining room creates a bow that is extended the entire height of the facade. On either side of the bow is an entrance portico of six Tuscan columns carrying an entablature with the hotel's emblem. Behind these entranceways, corridors run on either side of the main dining room to a wide corridor that connects entrances on the hotel's sides and forms the lobby. Behind that corridor is the vast ballroom and its foyer.

Now part of the Sheraton chain, the hotel is currently being refurbished according to its original period, and so will continue to give Bostonians and their visitors a feeling for Gilded Age grandeur.

Boston, Massachusetts   *Henry J. Hardenbergh, Architect*

THE COPLEY PLAZA

6
Clubs

*N*o other type of building was so transformed
from inconspicuousness to grandeur by
*Gilded Age architects as was the private club. The
splendor of that era's structures has become so
closely associated with the private club that clubs
being formed today will very often seek out old
Gilded Age mansions to convert into headquarters.*

*Despite the trend of that past period, some clubs
wanted to remain inconspicuous. The conservative
Philadelphia Club, founded in 1834, retains its 1838
clubhouse to this day, and when the building was enlarged in 1905-1906 by no less than Horace Trumbauer, the addition was in the same humble style as
the older section. True propriety, however, does not
necessarily reject real grandeur; in 1909–1911, the
equally conservative Union League of Philadelphia*

*built from the designs of Trumbauer a vast, palatial
classical addition to John Fraser's 1864–1865
Victorian structure.*

*New York clubs were on the whole the most re-
splendent of all, and this was largely due, as was
much that was great in New York construction during
the Gilded Age, to the architectural firm of McKim,
Mead and White. Although, of course, other grand
clubhouses in that and other cities were produced by
other architects, McKim, Mead and White created
so many fine clubs, and influenced the design of so
many more, that a large proportion of the structures
shown in this chapter are theirs.*

Newport Casino

Newport, Rhode Island

McKim, Mead and White, *Architects*

The best of all shingle style buildings is the Newport Casino. Erected in 1879–1881 from the designs of McKim, Mead and White, the Casino was built for James Gordon Bennett, publisher of the New York *Herald*. Bennett's guest, a Captain Candy, part of a visiting British polo team, was riding by the Reading Room, a Newport club, when a club member challenged him to ride his pony into the building. Candy obliged, and the governors of the Reading Room withdrew his privileges. Bennett thought himself insulted, and decided to build a club of his own. The new club was not much of a success, but its building was, and stands today as an important center of Newport life.

Beneath a long, pitched roof from which richly decorated gables emerge, a shingled second story held many of the club facilities. This floor is rarely opened today. To help pay for the building's maintenance, a row of eight small stores were placed on the first story along Bellevue Avenue. The stores, which are used to this day, each have a bay window for display, and are separated in the facade from adjoining stores by single brick piers. At the center of the row is a wide arch, leading to the entrance to the club rooms and to the central court.

The court is formed by the front section, the ells at that section's ends, and the curving piazza that connects the rear of those wings. The court originally contained a lawn and a fountain; today it holds a permanent tennis court. The piazza section of the southern ell has been enclosed to house a tennis museum. A restaurant, with a piazza overlooking the court, is housed in the northern ell; this section once had an upper floor, which burned long ago and was never replaced. One of the finest pleasures of Newport is a lunch on the restaurant piazza while viewing the court with its bulky tower that bears a Tiffany clock. Behind the main block of the building are additional tennis courts and a theater.

The Casino draws on Queen Anne, medieval, and even Japanese precedents. The modernists claim it as a precedent for their own architecture; they flatter themselves, for, while the theory behind both the shingle style and the modern may be similar, the products of the styles are not. In fact, in its symmetry and rich decoration, the Casino foretells the grandeur the Gilded Age was to come to expect, and so can be seen as a precedent for the classicism about to appear. But the shingle style is itself, and the Casino itself, and sight can prove it beautiful even without help from the intellect.

Newport, Rhode Island   *McKim, Mead and White, Architects*
NEWPORT CASINO

NEWPORT CASINO—COURT TOWER

NEWPORT CASINO—HORSESHOE PLAZA

Century Association

New York, New York

McKim, Mead and White, *Architects*

The close relationship between architecture, sculpture, and mural painting was recognized by the Gilded Age, and this relationship reveals itself solely through architecture in the facade of the Century Association in New York City. Because the clubhouse is wedged between other buildings, the facade becomes a flat canvas on which to paint in stone. Across the facade runs the brushstrokes of minutely carved bands. The Palladian loggia of the second floor is in itself an intricate piece of sculpture.

Stanford White, the architect of the 1889 structure, was a personal friend of sculptors and painters; professionally, he aided them in obtaining commissions. He expressed architecturally his love of their crafts in the Century Association's facade, behind which he placed rooms of carefully sculpted interior space.

New York, New York   *McKim, Mead and White, Architects*

CENTURY ASSOCIATION

]146[

CENTURY ASSOCIATION—READING ROOM

CENTURY ASSOCIATION—DINING ROOM

Metropolitan Club
New York, New York

McKim, Mead and White, *Architects*

J. P. Morgan had so many partners that he knew what to do, as always. He organized a club—the Metropolitan Club—exclusively for them. The club-house, still standing today and occupied by the same club, was completed in 1896 from the plans of McKim, Mead and White, particularly White.

A conservative structure, it nevertheless expresses opulence in its balconies, elaborate frieze and cornice, and spectacular gate and courtyard. The interiors are studies in Gilded Age splendor. The building as a whole befits its purpose, patron, and designers.

New York, New York　　　　　*McKim, Mead and White, Architects*
METROPOLITAN CLUB

METROPOLITAN CLUB—LADIES' PRIVATE DINING ROOM

METROPOLITAN CLUB—LADIES' DINING ROOM

METROPOLITAN CLUB—BILLIARD ROOM

Racquet and Tennis Club
New York, New York
McKim, Mead and White *Architects*

RACQUET AND TENNIS CLUB—TENNIS COURTS

The 1898 clubhouse of the Racquet and Tennis Club remains standing and provides a refreshing change from the glass boxes that today take up most of that section of New York City's Park Avenue. The facade is a block long, running from Fifty-second to Fifty-third Street. A row of 11 small arches line the ground story of the facade; the center arch contains the main entrance. Above the ground floor, two-story arched windows have on either side a lower and an upper line of four rectangular windows. The top floor presents a row of 11 blind arches, and is crested by a balustrade.

The interior contains such large areas as the tennis courts and the plunge of the Turkish bath. Neither inside nor out does size hamper the grace of McKim, Mead and White's design, and it seems little wonder that tennis, which the club was founded to promote, may be on its way to being more popular than croquet.

New York, New York　　　　*McKim, Mead and White, Architects*
RACQUET AND TENNIS CLUB

University Club

New York, New York

McKim, Mead and White, *Architects*

The University Club, built in 1897–1899, was designed by Charles Follen McKim, of McKim, Mead and White, in the style of an Italian Renaissance palazzo.

A three-tiered structure with rusticated walls and arched windows, it bears sculptured seals of various colleges of which its members are alumni. Interior decoration includes mural painting by Harry Siddons Mowbray in both the Council Room and the library.

The clubhouse is to be noted not only for its beautiful design, but also for the care expended in its construction.

New York, New York　　　　　*McKim, Mead and White, Architects*

UNIVERSITY CLUB

University Club—Library

New York Yacht Club

New York, New York

Warren and Wetmore, *Architects*

One of the most splendid and creative of club-houses is that which Whitney Warren, of Warren and Wetmore, designed for the New York Yacht Club. The club, sponsors of the America's Cup Race, was organized in 1844, incorporated in 1865, and moved from their old clubhouse at 67 Madison Avenue to their new home at 37 West Forty-fourth Street in January 1901.

In the French Renaissance facade, the entrance is set to one side; this unconventional asymmetry provides greater freedom in arranging the inner space allowed by a city lot. An especially notable feature of the facade is the three bay windows, fashioned after those of seventeenth-century Dutch vessels; these windows rise to round-arch windows that are Warren's trademark.

The most important interior is the Model Room, which is filled with replicas of yachts that have been registered with the club over the years. The room contains a 45-ton fireplace with a cresting of four arched sea serpents. The fireplace is made of Caen stone, which also covers the walls of many of the structure's interiors.

How perfectly the building is fitted to the honored organization that occupies it. The purpose and spirit of the club are expressed in this structure with a grace and suitability that only classical architecture has at its command.

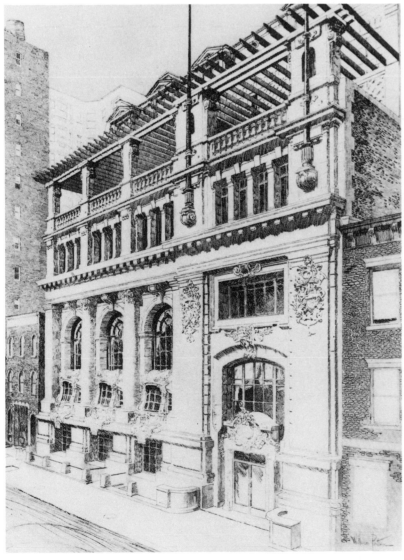

New York, New York *Warren and Wetmore, Architects*
NEW YORK YACHT CLUB

NEW YORK YACHT CLUB—DETAIL OF WINDOW

Colony Club

New York, New York

McKim, Mead and White, *Architects*

The fine, delicate interiors of the Colony Club, a women's organization, were the work of Elsie de Wolfe, the legendary woman decorator, and were important in advancing her career. After the club moved to new headquarters further uptown, the old building became the home of the American Academy of Dramatic Arts, which greatly altered the interior. Stanford White's dignified exterior for the 1902 building, however, remains intact.

Two windows are on each side of the arched doorway. Tall, thin composite columns support a balcony, onto which open, at the first floor level, five doors in relieving arches. Five windows on the second story correspond in position to those doors, and likewise five dormers are found in the pitched roof behind a cleverly carved balustrade.

New York, New York   *McKim, Mead and White, Architects*

COLONY CLUB

Pittsburgh Athletic Association

Pittsburgh, Pennsylvania

Jansson and Abbott, *Architects*

The Pittsburgh Athletic Association was founded in 1908, and it opened in 1911 the spectacular building by the fledgling architectural firm, Jansson and Abbott.

Pairs of composite pilasters surround the first two floors of the building, each pair of pilasters separated from the next by an arched window or door, with a medallion in every spandrel, and by a rectangular upper window with elaborate decoration at its sides. Above an entablature and a cornice that acts as a stringcourse is one two-story engaged composite column for each pilaster below, except at the building's corners, where the pilasters repeat. Separating any one pair of columns from any other are third- and fourth-floor rectangular windows in handsome frames. A frieze, broken by small windows, presents garlands and cherubs, and supports an ornate cornice. A porte-cochère extends from one end of the building across a semicircular driveway.

The first floor interior of the structure was decorated by Albert Herter, who also painted the dining room murals, now removed. The club continues to occupy the building, and has altered the interior for current activities, although such features as the lobby and the swimming pool, with its Guastavino tiles, remain intact.

Pittsburgh, Pennsylvania   *Jansson and Abbott, Architects*

PITTSBURGH ATHLETIC ASSOCIATION

7
Railroad Stations

"*The Gateways to the Cities*"—in this way were railroad stations often described during the Gilded Age.

Today, when long-distance passenger travel by rail seems a thing of the past, it is difficult to realize the fascination the people of that earlier era had with railroads. Because the drama of railroading was visible all around, no other industry held the public's interest so tightly. The railroad families, such as the Vanderbilts and the Goulds, were the celebrities of the times, and their private cars and private fortunes were everywhere discussed.

Neither had our cities yet fallen into disrepute.

While many of the conditions in them were the same then as they are now, the cities were not viewed as problems, set among glass and concrete boxes, but wonders, staged amidst classical and Gothic splendors. The cities were the glory of American civilization, not the bane of it.

And so only a structure of the greatest grandeur would be suitable to connect the pride of American living, which was the cities, with the pride of American industry, which was the railroads.

Reading Terminal

Philadelphia, Pennsylvania

Francis Kimball, *Architect of the Head House*
Wilson Brothers and Company, *Architects of the
Train Shed*

Constructed in 1892–1893, this passenger terminal of the Philadelphia and Reading Railroad was worthy of its perfectionist president, Angus
Archibald MacLeod, whose splendid private railroad
car is illustrated later in these pages. The Italian
Renaissance head house, designed by Francis Kimball,
has a first level of pink granite and upper stories of
pink brick trimmed with white terra-cotta tile icing.
A frothier confection cannot be imagined, especially
considering that the structure was intended to serve
as headquarters for what MacLeod envisioned as a
future railroad empire, extending up through all
New England. The ground floor of the building
contained such areas as an entrance lobby, ticket
office, and baggage rooms, while the second level
held dining and waiting rooms. Above these stories
were the management offices, including the president's
office with its corner bay window.

The second level provided passenger access to the
train shed, for which Wilson Brothers and Company
were the architects. Although few train sheds remain
today, these buildings designed specifically to house
entire trains were common during the Gilded Age. At
the time of its construction, Reading Terminal possessed the world's largest single-span shed; it mea-
sures 266 feet, 6 inches wide, and 559 feet long. At
street level beneath the trains is the famed Reading
Terminal Market, where a large number of booths
sold the finest foods.

Although the railroad, now called the Reading, is
still an important line, it never became the empire
of which MacLeod dreamed; the terminal now stands
in the worst part of center-city Philadelphia; and even
the Market today has many unoccupied booths. In
1948, over a million dollars was spent on a gloomy
modernization program that ruined the appearance
of the interior of the head house's passenger facilities, and the lower floors of the head house exterior.
Nevertheless, the upper exterior of the head house
remains cheerful in its grim surroundings, and to see
the mammoth shed looming ahead as one approaches
by train is always a dramatic experience.

Philadelphia, Pennsylvania   Francis Kimball, *Architect of the Head House*
Wilson Brothers and Company, *Architects of the Train Shed*
READING TERMINAL

Graver's Lane Station

Philadelphia, Pennsylvania

Furness, Evans and Company, *Architects*

A grander train station to illustrate the work of Frank Furness, of Furness, Evans and Company, would be the Pennsylvania Railroad's medieval-style Broad Street Station, which stood beside Philadelphia City Hall from 1880 to 1954. Perhaps more typical of buildings by Furness is the little Graver's Lane Station, built around 1886, which still stands on the Chestnut Hill branch of the Reading, then Philadelphia and Reading, Railroad.

Frank Furness, like Chicago's Louis Sullivan, re-fused to adopt the traditional styles that flourished in the Gilded Age; Furness, until his death in 1912, stuck to the romantic design of years before. His works are currently enjoying a great vogue, particularly in Philadelphia, his home city, among modern architects, who understand the similarity between romantic and modern architectural theory, and whose own training stressed "originality" (not to be confused with "creativity"). Today, the observer not steeped in the history of architecture finds buildings by Furness either quaint or absurd. The people of the architect's own day shared this opinion, and they were right. It seems most artists who fly undaunted into the face of convention ought not to.

Philadelphia, Pennsylvania   *Furness, Evans and Company, Architects*
GRAVER'S LANE STATION

Union Station

Pittsburgh, Pennsylvania

Daniel H. Burnham, *Architect*

The Pennsylvania State Main Line of Public Works began operation in 1828; a series of canals, railroads, and inclined planes, it was designed to carry the passenger between Philadelphia and Pittsburgh in only four days. In 1854, the first through train service was inaugurated by the Pennsylvania Railroad; the scheduled duration of the journey was thirteen to seventeen hours. Eight hours was the average time for the trip by 1902, the year the new Union Station opened in Pittsburgh.

Daniel H. Burnham, who designed the new station, had gained his reputation as the chief architect for the World's Columbian Exposition in Chicago in 1893, an event that was singularly important in the history of American architecture (and is explored earlier in this volume). The new station greatly derived from the festival atmosphere of the fair, the station's rotunda being the special heir. Burnham had included a rather prosaic cabstand in the rotunda's place when he made his original plan, which he drew up in 1899; by the time the station was finished, however, considerable changes had been made in his design. The office building was greatly heightened; it held on the upper floors the offices of the Western Division of the Pennsy, and on the ground level, the waiting room and other public areas. The growth of the rotunda was a masterful addition to the plan. While the exterior of the stone structure presents a light-hearted facade to the Golden Triangle, the interior is a grotto of ever-changing shapes in light and shade, caused by the wide arches. If railroad stations were the Gateways to the Cities, this Gateway has a fascinating gateway all its own.

Pittsburgh, Pennsylvania   *Daniel H. Burnham, Architect*

UNION STATION

UNION STATION, PITTSBURGH—ROTUNDA

UNION STATION, PITTSBURGH, BY NIGHT

PENNSYLVANIA STATION—CONCOURSE

Philadelphia, Pennsylvania   *Edgar V. Seeler, Architect*

CURTIS PUBLISHING COMPANY

In the foreground is the steeple of Independence Hall.

Boston, Massachusetts *Edward H. Sears, Architect*
RESIDENCE OF MRS. ISABELLA STEWART GARDNER—COURT

Pennsylvania Station
New York, New York
McKim, Mead and White, *Architects*

A t the turn of the century, a ride from Philadelphia to New York over the mighty Pennsylvania Railroad ended in a ferry ride. The trains
terminated in the gigantic shed at Jersey City, then
the passengers rode a railroad company Red Star
Line ferry across the Hudson to Manhattan. In the
beginning of the twentieth century, though, the railroad, under the leadership of its daring president,
Alexander J. Cassatt, employed Clifford Holland,
who gave his name to his new automobile tunnel, to
ferret beneath the Hudson a tunnel for trains.
Charles Follen McKim, of McKim, Mead and
White, was commissioned to design a station in New
York City befitting this great endeavor. From his

designs was built in 1906–1910 o
railroad stations ever erected in t
The tracks into the station were s
track level was reached through han
from the concourse, an amazing inter
metal. The concourse adjoined an
room, the Great Hall. In this space o
portions, majestic Corinthian columns s
a vast coffered ceiling.
In an irresponsible and heartless decisio
structure was demolished in 1964 to make
insipid present Madison Square Garden.
the decoration was saved, such as the eagles
adorn the site of the new Garden and the
Street Bridge in Philadelphia, but by and la
sculpture and other ornaments are now broken
in a dumping pile on the New Jersey marshes,
ported there through the tunnel that they orig
celebrated.

New York, New York *McKim, Mead and White, Architects*
PENNSYLVANIA STATION

]161[

PENNSYLVANIA STATION—GREAT HALL

Union Station

Washington, District of Columbia

Daniel H. Burnham, *Architect*

As Union Station in Pittsburgh demonstrates, the World's Columbian Exposition, held at Chicago in 1893, had strong influence on American architecture. When the McMillan Commission was established in Washington in 1901 to bring order to that city's then-haphazard growth, the Exposition was drawn upon heavily. The previous Washington terminal of the Pennsylvania Railroad had been east of the Capitol, actually on the Mall, a site it shared with numerous shacks and a swamp. So that the Mall could be developed into the present park, a new station was erected in 1908 to the north of the Capitol. The architect was, as for the Pittsburgh station, Daniel H. Burnham, who had been chief architect for the Exposition, and his impressive Roman station at Washington showed the suitability of the Exposition style for gracing the nation's capital city, and for complementing its neighbor, the Capitol Building.

The central section of the facade of the Vermont granite terminal includes six Ionic columns, two at each end of that part of the facade, and two single columns separating three tall round arches. Above each column, upon the cornice, stands one of six 18-foot figures, representing Fire and Electricity, Agriculture and Mechanics, and Freedom and Imagination; these statues are the work of Louis St. Gaudens. Extending from the sides of the central section are wings, each bearing seven smaller arches, and each terminating in a pavilion, through the arches of which taxicabs and other automobiles can pass to pick up and deliver passengers. Both the waiting room and concourse are immense, and reflective of the Roman architecture that inspired the station. The trains arrive on 30 tracks at the rear of the terminal, alongside canopied platforms running perpendicular to the front of the structure.

Union Station in Washington was the first heir of the McMillan Commission, which in turn inherited much from the Chicago Exposition. The terminal is an elegant herald of the beauty both Exposition and Commission were to will to the city of Washington of today.

Washington, District of Columbia   *Daniel H. Burnham, Architect*

UNION STATION

UNION STATION, WASHINGTON—MAIN WAITING ROOM

Grand Central Terminal

New York, New York

Warren and Wetmore, *Architects*

The nation that built Grand Central Terminal need not envy Europe in matters of architectural quality.

Whitney Warren, of Warren and Wetmore, designed the building in 1910 for the great New York Central Railroad. A low platform comprises the ground level that contains stores and entrances to the station and supports the upper elevations, which are recessed behind automobile ramps. Due to a fall in the terrain, the ground story is hidden from view more than two blocks away down Park Avenue, which axis the front of the station closes at Forty-second Street. The facade contains three gigantic window bays, separated by double pairs of Roman Doric columns.

Crowning the station is the monumental sculpture group by Jules-Alexis Coutan. Resting upon the broken round pediment, containing a clock and some of the floral ornaments found throughout the facade, are Hercules, or Physcial Energy on the left, and Minerva, or Moral Energy on the right. Mercury, the god of commerce and science (and thievery) is between them; that figure is 28 feet high. Behind him is a national symbol, the eagle.

Directly below the Mercury group, at the base of the facade, stands a bronze statue by A. de Groot of Commodore Vanderbilt, the founder of the railroad line. The figure was once the center of a copper relief on the pediment of the St. John's Park Freight Terminal in lower Manhattan. When that terminal was torn down in 1936, the statue was moved to its present site.

Trains destined for Grand Central Terminal go underground at 97th Street and Park Avenue, and continue under the avenue (which, in fact, was created when the New York Central covered its tracks) until they halt on one of the station's vast number of tracks. The engineers for the complicated system of tracks, ramps, and levels were William J. Wilgus and the firm of Reed and Stem.

The suburban rider will most often emerge into the lower of the two pedestrian levels. This is a series of dramatic vaults, finished in tile. When he climbs to the upper level where long-distance trains arrive, he will behold the huge main hall. On the curved blue ceiling decorated by Paul Helleu, the traveler will see constellations, the stars represented by electric lights and connected with white delineations of the mythological subjects. Alternating with the dentils surrounding the ceiling are incandescent bulbs; in this feature, classical design demonstrates how well it can incorporate modern invention. If the observer goes through the connecting modern intruder, Walter Gropius's Pan American Airlines Building, he will come to the New York General Building, one of America's most lavish office buildings. Described later in these pages, it is also the work of Whitney Warren, and was designed, with the title the New York Central Building, to house the main offices of that railway.

Manhattan's other great train station, Pennsylvania Station, was destroyed in 1964, and Grand Central Terminal may soon be torn down and replaced with a modern office building. Failing that, there has been a proposal to erect an office building above the roof of the terminal. Public-spirited citizens and even architects (the group usually last to take up the cause of architectural conservation) are working to keep Grand Central Terminal as it is. But it remains to be seen if the present age thinks itself worthy of having great architecture in its midst.

New York, New York *Warren and Wetmore, Architects*
GRAND CENTRAL TERMINAL

GRAND CENTRAL TERMINAL—GREAT HALL

]167[

8
Stores

The love of making money, a characteristic of the Gilded Age (and no other?), would have gone unrequited but for an equally characteristic passion for spending it. The merchants of the era realized for the first time that a product could be sold not only on its own qualities, but also through its surroundings. In a period of grand architecture, it was easy to create a beautiful aura for buying, and the architectural aspects of salesmanship were brought to bear earlier than packaging, advertising, and industrial design, all of which advanced during the Gilded Age.

The Gilded Age's love of giganticism was manifest in the development of the department store. There had been department stores before that era, but those were simply stores that sold a lot of different things. The Gilded Age conceived the department store of today, where practically every item needed in daily life is available in a self-contained city of selling.

Outside the department store, the specialty shop continued, but in an elegant new building. Then there was that new creation, the five-and-ten. Today's stores, like much else in America, are the gift of the Gilded Age.

A Row of Shops

Newport, Rhode Island

Many small shops from the Gilded Age are still being used today; the famous row of stores along the east side of Bellevue Avenue in Newport, which was designed by some of that earlier period's greatest architects, is still in service.

The Travers Block, designed by Richard Morris Hunt, was built around 1875 to provide much-needed stores for the expanding summer colony. A two-and-a half-story building, it has shops along the street and bachelor quarters above. The Travers Block is in the stick style, extremely popular at the time, and has a vast mansard roof. It stands on land won by William R. Travers from the owner of a gambling house at the rear. A condition of the bet was, should Travers win, that a small footpath had to be kept open to the gambling house, no matter what was built on the disputed land; the passageway can still be used today.

The Newport Casino, by McKim, Mead and White, contains eight stores that help pay for the maintenance of the building. The structure, which is discussed in detail earlier in this book, was erected in 1879–1881, and was soon after joined to the south by a new, smaller complementary building, mainly for shops.

Yet another structure, the Audrain Building, erected in 1902 from the designs of Bruce Price, is the last building of the old row. Six gigantic bays on the facade, and one at each end of the structure, open on stores at the first story and offices on the second. Access to the offices is gained through a ground-floor door, which, together with a slim, upper-story arch, divides the wide arches of the facade into groups of three. The arches and cornice are trimmed in polychrome tile, which makes for a spectacular sight on a very sunny day.

The row is still used by some of Newport's finest shops, the quality of the architecture enhancing the quality of the merchandise.

TRAVERS BLOCK

AUDRAIN BUILDING

NEWPORT CASINO
The bay window at the center of the facade was replaced by a loggia soon after the clubhouse was completed.

Charles Scribner's Sons

New York, New York

Ernest Flagg, *Architect*

Ernest Flagg designed two successive headquarters for Charles Scribner's Sons, the famous publishing house founded in 1846 at New York City. The first of their buildings by Flagg, 153 Fifth Avenue at Twenty-first Street, was occupied by Scribner's from 1894 to 1913, when the firm moved to the second, 597 Fifth Avenue at Forty-eighth, the company's present home. Each structure was built with a bookstore on the ground level and offices above.

The newer building was necessitated by lack of space, and many of the features of the six-story older structure were lovingly retained in the newer, which has twice as many stories. The facade of the bookstores on the first level of both buildings are of iron, the newer store having a greater amount of glass to admit additional natural light. Both stores have a rusticated story above the bookstore, then a number of stories closely related to each other, and topped off with a mansard roof.

The earlier of these buildings was erected at the beginning of the City Beautiful movement, and the other at the movement's peak. On a sunlit day, when one enters the delicately decorated bookstore of blue and white with balconies behind handsome black railings, one realizes what today's cities might have looked like, had not that movement been stopped in its tracks in favor of bleak modernism.

New York, New York   *Ernest Flagg, Architect*
CHARLES SCRIBNER'S SONS, 153 FIFTH AVENUE

New York, New York   *Ernest Flagg, Architect*
CHARLES SCRIBNER'S SONS, 597 FIFTH AVENUE

CHARLES SCRIBNER'S SONS, 597 FIFTH AVENUE—BOOKSTORE

Schlesinger and Mayer
Chicago, Illinois
Louis H. Sullivan, *Architect*

Louis Sullivan is a darling of the modernists, because his buildings anticipate modern architecture. The modernists consider their style the only true faith, and since Sullivan was its prophet, he was therefore a great architect. A more rational age than the present may have doubts about the qualities of modern architecture and those of Sullivan. Next to the work of architects in the mainstream of Gilded Age design, his buildings appear plain at best, or more often, bizarre or offensive or just plain silly.

Probably his most admirable building was the Schlesinger and Mayer Department Store in Chicago. It was built in 1899 with additions in 1903–1904 (and later additions by other architects). The first two stories are bedecked with Sullivan's weird decoration, which is one of his trademarks. His decoration is beloved of the modernists because it is original—not the same old beautiful classical stuff—and originality is a goal of modern architecture, right down to the present ironclad rule of absolutely no decoration on buildings (which is certainly original, since every other architectural period from cave dwelling times has decorated its surroundings). The upper stories of the building are just about unadorned, with big Chicago windows with peculiar little decoration around them. The cornice that this building once possessed has been removed, as have the festoons between pairs of second-story windows.

Carson Pirie Scott and Company department store moved into the building in 1904 and have continued to occupy it to the present, so the building is better known by their name than by that of its previous resident. The partners Carson and Pirie came to this country in 1854 from Northern Ireland, and moved almost immediately to Illinois. Each married the other's sister. The brothers Scott joined the firm in 1856 after emigrating from the same country. The business was a regulation Gilded Age success story, and is one of Chicago's finest department stores. The building is a symbol of the Chicago school, whatever one thinks of that; and whatever one thinks of the building, it is far better than the present-day construction it helped create.

SCHLESINGER AND MAYER—MAIN ENTRANCE

Chicago, Illinois   *Louis H. Sullivan, Architect*

SCHLESINGER AND MAYER

John Wanamaker

Philadelphia, Pennsylvania

Daniel H. Burnham, *Architect*

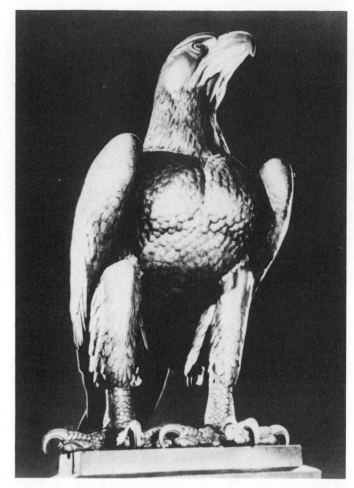

JOHN WANAMAKER—BRONZE EAGLE

America's most beautiful department store is Philadelphia's John Wanamaker, a building designed by Daniel H. Burnham. Chief architect of the World's Columbian Exposition held in Chicago in 1893, Burnham knew better than anybody how to endow a building with gaiety and adventure. He made Wanamaker's an absolutely splendid place for people to spend their money and have fun doing it.

In commissioning Burnham, the company's founder must have realized the importance of the setting to the selling, but John Wanamaker was always a pioneer in merchandising. Born 11 July 1838, in a decade that saw the births of many Gilded Age tycoons, he grew up to make early success in retailing menswear. In 1875, he bought a freight depot from the Pennsylvania Railroad and opened two years later in that structure "The New Kind of Store," a department store. The business grew to cover an entire block, and on 11 July 1904 construction of the present structure began. When completed, the building contained 45 acres of floor space. President Taft officially dedicated the building on 30 December 1911. Eleven years later, Wanamaker was taken ill at his office in the store, and returned home, forgetting his hat. He died 12 December 1922; his office remains to this day as he left it, with his hat still on his desk.

Burnham's building, like its predecessor, covers an entire block. Two-story Doric columns are at some of the present building's entrances, which are found on each side of the structure. Piers of the same height surround the rest of the building. Above rest seven floors of rusticated walls, and above that, the remaining floors with smooth walls. Stringcourses separate the different sections of wall, and the building is crowned by a wide cornice.

The most important interior feature is the Grand Court, which rises at the building's center through the first eight floors. Wanamaker's regularly schedules events in the hall, including organ recitals every working day. The great organ was originally designed by George Ashdown Audsley and built by the Los Angeles Art Organ Company for the Louisiana Purchase Exposition in St. Louis during 1904. It has been enlarged, and now has a six manual console, 451 stops, and 30,067 working pipes, although the pipes shown here are for decoration alone. Another souvenir of the same fair is the majestic bronze eagle by August Gaul of Berlin. "Meet me at the eagle" is a phrase well known to Philadelphians; the person who arrives early will enjoy waiting in one of Philadelphia's greatest interior spaces.

All the public areas are enriched with architectural decoration, and often with paintings. The Greek Hall is a delicate classical room for smaller gatherings; for large numbers, there is an auditorium in the Egyptian style, found sparsely sprinkled throughout the history of American architecture. The Crystal Tea Room creates great elegance with its oak paneling and its crystal chandeliers.

Mosaics at the entrances and graceful iron staircases all combine to give Wanamaker's a special place in Philadelphia life and American architecture. Fortunately, the store's management realizes the building's greatness, and do not try to remodel away the beauty the brilliant Burnham gave the store.

Philadelphia, Pennsylvania   *Daniel H. Burnham, Architect*

JOHN WANAMAKER

JOHN WANAMAKER—GRAND COURT

9
Office Buildings

The Gilded Age created big business. Before the epoch, business had been carried on generally at a personal level; office buildings were often converted residences, although relatively small buildings were sometimes erected especially for offices. But big companies required big headquarters. The Gilded Age answered the need with the period's stimulating architecture, able to express the wealth and power of big business. The steel frame was many times combined with the elevator to produce the first skyscrapers, the homes of vertical corporations. Business was the pride of Gilded Age life, as the office buildings of the era give eloquent evidence.

Witherspoon Building

Philadelphia, Pennsylvania

Joseph Huston, *Architect*

Sculpture was the companion of architecture until modern architecture stripped buildings of their decoration; the vast amount of sculpture that coats the exterior of the Witherspoon Building may help the structure meet the demand of modern theory that the appearance of a building reveal its use. The seals of Presbyterian organizations and statues and portrait medallions of Presbyterian ministers and laymen give a definite hint that the building was erected for the Presbyterian Board of Christian Education.

Joseph Huston designed the handsome classical building, which was erected in 1896. Alexander Stirling Calder was the sculptor of the six statues of divines above the entrances; Calder's father had designed the sculpture for the Philadelphia City Hall, which is pictured in this volume. The ten large biblical figures at the eighth floor are the work of Samuel Murray.

The modernists are not content to build barren buildings; they must also strip the buildings from the past of their lovely ornament. Accordingly, the building was modernized in 1961. All the statues were removed; the divines are now at the Presbyterian Historical Society in Philadelphia and eight of the biblical figures now decorate a graveyard in suburban Philadelphia, while the other two—Moses and Elijah —currently reside in Skagway, Alaska. The rest of the decoration remains on the walls, at least until the building is again visited by the modernists.

Philadelphia, Pennsylvania *Joseph Huston, Architect*

WITHERSPOON BUILDING

New York Stock Exchange
New York, New York

George Brown Post, *Architect*

The Wall Street area contains some of the finest classical architecture in America, and little wonder, since the section is the center of American financial activity and the classical style is so admirably suited to displaying the power of American business. The most famous of the district's buildings is the New York Stock Exchange, which George Brown Post designed in 1900.

The Broad Street facade is particularly impressive. A two-story base supports six huge Corinthian columns between a pair of pilasters. In the pediment is sculpture by J. Q. A. Ward and Paul W. Bartlett. An attic with a balustrade tops the facade. The Cor-

inthian order masks a gigantic glass wall; that window illuminates the building's most important room, the main trading room, which is of the largest size and the richest decoration, including the remarkable polychrome ceiling.

The false front is despised of modernists because it has no function, and similarly because it does away with the "truthfulness" of the structure. How a building can tell a lie is another question, but modernists are fond of attaching human virtues and vices to architecture. As for function, the false front seems to have a very important one; considering the importance of the business of the New York Stock Exchange, it is good the traders have this mighty, yet human edifice to remind them, as no cold, barren, modern structure could, that behind the powerful facade of finance stands the brittle aspirations of millions of people.

New York, New York   *George Brown Post, Architect*

NEW YORK STOCK EXCHANGE

Fuller Building
New York, New York

Daniel H. Burnham, *Architect*

There had been skyscrapers before the Flatiron Building, always the popular and now the correct name for the Fuller Building. Robert Mills's 1848–1885 Washington Monument in the nation's capital and the tower of John McArthur's 1871–1901 Philadelphia City Hall were taller, but these were towers and not inhabited buildings, although the City Hall tower had an inhabited building below it. Burnham and Root's Monadnock Building, erected in 1891 in Chicago, was an office building that succeeded in reaching 16 stories. All these earlier buildings were of masonry construction, with the walls supporting the buildings. While this made little difference with towers, it was impractical for other types of skyscrapers, because the walls had to be so thick at the bottom—six feet, in the case of the Monadnock Building. For great height, the answer was a frame of iron or, later, steel; the walls hung from the frame, allowing thin walls in buildings of great height. There had been other skyscrapers of this type

of construction before the Flatiron Building, but none reached the height, or so caught the country's attention, as did Daniel H. Burnham's masterpiece of 1902.

The building's site, formed by the intersection of Broadway and Fifth Avenue at Twenty-third Street, was called at the time of the building's construction, "a stingy piece of pie." Accordingly, the building narrows from 85 feet at one end to six at the other. Its foundations go down 35 feet, and the structure rises 307 feet above ground, or 21 stories.

Although the building announced a new age of construction technique, it did not warn of the coming day of undecorated blandness that was to be particularly apparent in the design of skyscrapers. The Flatiron Building's 3,680 tons of structural steel are hung with masonry walls, fabulously carved with intricate figures. The meaningless, but often-repeated argument of the modernists against decoration on skyscrapers is that people do not see it. Many people do not see, hear, or sense much of anything architectural or otherwise, but that does not mean decoration such as that on the Flatiron Building, the designs of which can be seen if the viewer wants to see them, should not beautify buildings.

New York, New York   *Daniel H. Burnham, Architect*

FULLER BUILDING

New York Central Building

New York, New York

Warren and Wetmore, *Architects*

Park Avenue is still a City Beautiful axis, closed at its center by Grand Central Terminal and its companion structure, the New York Central Building. Although many of the classical facades that lined the avenue have been replaced by glass boxes, the train station and the office building continue, for a time anyway, to testify to the grandeur of the plan, even though the pair are now separated by the backdrop of the immense but tedious Pan Am Building. The old office building has, by the modification of one letter and the change of another, had the "CENTRAL" of the name on its facade changed to "GENERAL," an alteration indicative of the plight of the New York Central and its merged form.

Whoever the occupants, the building remains a very successful adaptation of classical design to the American skyscraper. A wide lower section bends its sides gracefully forward. Two huge arches, the shapes of which are typical of the work of the building's architect Whitney Warren, receive or send forth automobiles from or to the ramp surrounding Grand Central Terminal. At the center of the lower section of the facade, a large rectangular entrance leads to an exquisite lobby of marble and bronze. Even the elevators are splendid; their red walls, trimmed with gold, rise to ceilings painted with clouds, ceilings that give the passenger the feeling of going heavenward when he is headed in that direction.

The facade's lower and upper sections are joined by sculpture and a clock. More than 20 stories lead up to a row of column shafts held against the facade by brackets. A slanting roof is crowned by a green and gold lantern.

The beauty of the 1913 New York Central Building gives pleasure not only to pedestrians and the people that work in it, but also to workers in surrounding buildings, who are refreshed by a glimpse of its delicate detail through the glass walls of the modern buildings in which they are confined.

NEW YORK CENTRAL BUILDING—DETAIL OF TERRA COTTA EXTERIOR DECORATION

New York, New York   *Warren and Wetmore, Architects*

NEW YORK CENTRAL BUILDING

NEW YORK CENTRAL BUILDING—LOBBY

Woolworth Building

New York, New York

Cass Gilbert, *Architect*

Frank W. Woolworth, born in 1852, left his parents' farm at age 21 to work in a retail store in Watertown, New York; at that store he heard of "The 5¢ Counter," and he soon opened a store of his own. Every item for sale there cost five cents, was displayed on a counter, and had to be paid for in cash. His first store was a failure, but his second, opened in Lancaster, Pennsylvania, when he was 27, was a great success. He soon included also dime items, and so created the world's first five-and-ten. By the time of his death in 1919, the Woolworth Company operated over a thousand stores. When constructing the Woolworth Building, the corporate headquarters designed by Cass Gilbert and opened in 1913, Woolworth, true to the policies of his stores, paid the $13,500,000 cost of the building in cash from his own fortune built on nickels and dimes.

The building is Gothic, a style that Americans closely connect with church architecture. Dr. S. Parkes Cadman, the famous New York clergyman, called the structure early in its existence a "Cathedral of Commerce," a name that stuck to the building ever since, along with the reflection by many people that the Gilded Age built more spectacular monuments to business than to God. While this belief has a good deal of truth in it, as revealed in this book's chapters on churches and banks, much of the wor-

shipfulness seen in the Woolworth Building results from insufficient separation of church and Gothic. Actually, the style has given the nation many great buildings of all uses, and ought to be allowed to continue to do so.

The delicate exterior rises to 792 feet of spires, flying buttresses, and traceries. Bas relief heads depicting Asia, Africa, Europe, and America are at the second story, and gargoyles at the twenty-sixth, forty-ninth, and fifty-first stories. And all this decoration is able to be seen by those who are willing to look.

The lobby is three stories high. The marble of the walls comes from Skyros; Commerce, and Labor are the subjects of a pair of frescoes on the second-floor balconies; the ceiling of glass mosaic is, like the rest of the lobby, lit by indirect lighting. The famous corbels caricature persons connected with the building's construction: Frank Woolworth is shown counting his coins.

The building has 60 stories, including the subterranean levels. There might have been 80 stories to the structure, but Woolworth insisted on high Gothic ceilings, none in the building being less than eleven feet. The quality of decoration is continued in every corridor.

From the time it was built to 1930, the Woolworth Building was the world's tallest occupied structure. How obvious it seemed then that, when building a landmark of engineering, the relatively little extra money should be spent to make it a landmark of architectural design.

WOOLWORTH BUILDING—CORBEL
Caricaturing Frank Woolworth counting his nickels and dimes.

New York, New York   *Cass Gilbert, Architect*

WOOLWORTH BUILDING

WOOLWORTH BUILDING—LOBBY

WOOLWORTH BUILDING UNDER CONSTRUCTION
Showing the steel frame that made skyscrapers possible

Curtis Publishing Company

Philadelphia, Pennsylvania

Edgar V. Seeler, *Architect*

The Curtis Publishing Company, which produced a number of magazines, including the *Saturday Evening Post,* opened a new headquarters in 1914 at the firm's home city of Philadelphia. The building is the finest product of its architect, Edgar V. Seeler.

The Curtis Building faces the square containing Independence Hall, where the nation was formed. Both the Curtis structure and its very similar companion, the Public Ledger Building, a newspaper office erected in 1924–1928 to the designs of Horace Trumbauer, were conceived as suitable neighbors to, but not backdrops for, that famous statehouse, which was built from 1730 to 1748 from plans by Edmund Woolley and Andrew Hamilton, with a steeple by William Strickland added in 1828.

The two-story white marble base of the Curtis Building is set off by a row of Ionic columns. This base carries a six-story brick section, which in turn bears a white marble top section with round-arch windows and a cresting balustrade.

The building's best feature is its lobby. A spacious, relatively low room, all its walls, floors, and ceiling are of pure white marble. Across from the entrance, behind a long fountain, is a wall-size glass mosaic. The scene is *The Dream Garden;* the work was executed by Tiffany Studios after a painting by Maxfield Parrish.

The Curtis Publishing Company now occupies only a small part of the building, which is still maintained in fine condition.

A current problem in business seems to be the employee who feels himself part of a machine. A present-day businessman, before constructing one more modern edifice, the design of which both he and his architect falsely believe to be "scientific," would do well to visit the Curtis Building, and consider whether workers in such a building think themselves mechanized or unimportant.

Philadelphia, Pennsylvania   *Edgar V. Seeler, Architect*

CURTIS PUBLISHING COMPANY

In the foreground is the steeple of Independence Hall; the Public Ledger Building is to the right.

10
Banks

No doubt about it: the Gilded Age was devoted to money. As often noted, the age decorated its banks more lavishly than its churches.

Bona fide excuses can be made for this phenomenon. The banks were nearly always classical, which lends itself easier to rich ornament than does Gothic, the style of nearly all the churches. Furthermore, Protestant America has always valued simplicity in churches on religious principles.

But these apologies, accurate though they may be, cannot hide the pleasure the period took in dressing its banks as elaborate pagan temples. Fortunately for the souls of the era, the Gilded Age was sufficiently well-to-do that if God and mammon could not simultaneously be served, they could at least peacefully coexist.

Bowery Savings Bank
New York, New York
McKim, Mead and White, *Architects*

The Bowery was originally an Indian path, then a route through Dutch farms, *bouwerie* meaning "farm" in Dutch. Later it was a center for New York fashion, then a center for immigrants, and is today a slum. The Bowery Savings Bank opened for business in 1834; Hamilton Fish and Peter G. Stuyvesant were two of the trustees. On the bank's original site, the new building by McKim, Mead and White opened in 1894, construction having started in the previous year.

The building is majestic with its Corinthian columns and pilasters, with pediments each containing sculpture and a clock and bearing acroteria. The interia decoration is extremely rich, as typified by the coffered ceiling with its huge square light.

The edifice is today no longer the single office of the bank, but a branch; the newer headquarters at Forty-second Street is illustrated in the last chapter of this book. The photographs seen here show the older bank as it is today, one of the countless legacies inadvertently left to the poor by the rich that fashion has forced to leave noble neighborhoods for dull modern environments.

New York, New York　　　　　　*McKim, Mead and White, Architects*
BOWERY SAVINGS BANK

BOWERY SAVINGS BANK—CEILING

Riggs National Bank

Washington, District of Columbia

York and Sawyer, *Architects*

No doubt about it: this building is a bank. From 1880 all the time down to 1950, the Roman temple was almost automatically assumed to be the fittest form for a bank building. The reason why so many banks took after Roman temples is unknown; probably the Roman temple for use as a bank was first conceived because it suggested the majesty, wealth, solemnity, austerity, dignity, and so on, that banks then wanted to display, and the connection between design and use simply caught on and was perpetuated by the conservatism of bankers. Whatever the reason for the connection, almost every Gilded Age architectural firm was called upon at one time or another to plan a Roman temple for a bank.

Some of the designs were great, as other banks shown in this chapter demonstrate, and most designs were at least good, helped by the usual advantages of the classical style and the relatively large amounts of money available for construction.

The Riggs National Bank at 1503 Pennsylvania Avenue, N. W., in Washington, is slightly better than the average Gilded Age bank building, but all the same a good example of the general type. It was built in 1898 from the designs of York and Sawyer, who partly specialized in banks. The pair of Ionic columns and their enclosing walls support the entablature and pediment. The large upper window and first-floor entrance, which are enclosed in the portico, were repeated in a later addition to the left by a similar window and, on the first story, a small window. The pedimental sculpture, cornice, entablature, and door frame are boldly carved to give the bank building an uncommon vigor.

Washington, District of Columbia　　　　　　*York and Sawyer, Architects*
Riggs National Bank

Riggs National Bank—Main Banking Room

Girard Trust Company

Philadelphia, Pennsylvania

McKim, Mead and White, *Architects*

The rich little old lady from suburban Philadelphia is said to pray every night for the Republican Party, the Pennsylvania Railroad, and the Girard Bank. The third of these institutions was founded in 1836 and is named in honor of Stephen Girard, but not a descendant of his bank. The present home of the Girard Bank was erected in 1907–1908 under the bank presidency of Effingham B. Morris, and is the noble structure the noble bank deserves.

The square building of white marble presents six Ionic columns to Broad Street. The columns support an entablature, the pediment of which contains the image of Girard, surrounded by the ships that gathered his fortune. A similar, but less prominent, arrangement of four columns and plain pediment, is on the Chestnut Street side. A dome, smooth on the exterior, swells at the building's top, with an oculus that admits light to the large, ornate banking room beneath, where the little old lady is accommodated.

Philadelphia, Pennsylvania   McKim, Mead and White, Architects
GIRARD TRUST COMPANY

GIRARD TRUST COMPANY—MAIN BANKING ROOM

Brooklyn Trust Company, Main Office

Brooklyn, New York

York and Sawyer, *Architects*

One of the best of York and Sawyer's many bank buildings was the main office of the Brooklyn Trust Company and is now, through consolidation, the Brooklyn Heights Branch of the Manufacturers Hanover Trust Company.

The limestone building built in 1913 occupies a long, narrow site at the end of a block. The first story and apparent mezzanine are rusticated and vermiculated, with a row of arched windows along the exposed side and an arched entrance at each end. Above a Vitruvian scroll rises two stories, surrounded by engaged Corinthian columns that support an entablature and cornice. Marvelous details, such as the lamps and the gates give a hint of the splendor within.

Offices occupy the top two stories, and the main banking room the first level, the coffered vault of the ceiling descending to the mezzanine height revealed by the stringcourse on the exterior. From the ceiling hang chandeliers, each with an upper and lower group of bulbs separated by caryatids. Delicate banking tables with cabriole legs stand upon the remarkable floor, inlaid with the marbles of several countries. The interior has been slightly modernized, but with much regard for the original beauty.

Ah, the fabled land of Brooklyn! Its name's comic connotations hampers notice of the beauty of many of its buildings, monuments, parks, and communities. Like all cities, it is rapidly going to seed, as its fashion-seeking inhabitants move to pink clapboard houses further up Long Island.

Brooklyn, New York   *York and Sawyer, Architects*

BROOKLYN TRUST COMPANY

BROOKLYN TRUST COMPANY—MAIN BANKING ROOM

11
Churches

*I*f the Gilded Age was deeply concerned with money, the age was also highly concerned with religion. J. P. Morgan, attending a convention of Episcopal bishops at Richmond, Virginia, when the 1907 panic hit Wall Street, was begged by numerous telegrams to come home, but was too interested in the conference to leave before its close. At its conclusion, he returned to New York, and over a few days solved the Street's problem.

And if the Gilded Age generally built its churches less grand than its banks, the age still built some magnificent churches that could best any bank. The Gothic style, which had become popular in this country for buildings of all uses during the Romantic Era, was retained for Gilded Age churches; for a period struggling to acquire a European outlook, it seemed only natural to build churches in the style of the most famous European cathedrals. The Gilded Age is not remembered as an active period of church construction, since many important churches from colonial and federal times continued to be adequate for Gilded Age needs and had already come to be appreciated for their beauty. But many churches were built, particularly the churches in communities then new and the large cathedrals of cities.

Cathedral Church of St. John the Divine

New York, New York

George L. Heins and C. Grant LaFarge; Cram and Ferguson; and Others, *Architects*

The most important contribution of the Gilded Age to American church architecture was the construction of cathedrals comparable to the great medieval ones. While previous periods in American history had produced many impressive churches, some of very large proportions, it was not until the Gilded Age that structures of such gigantic size would be built. St. John the Divine, the cathedral of the Episcopal Diocese of New York, is one of the largest churches in Christendom.

Construction was begun in 1892, and halted in 1911 with two chapels and part of the crossing complete. The work was resumed in 1916, and continued sporadically to 1941, after which there has been no major construction. Completed during the second period were the apsidal chapels, the nave, the west front (except for the towers), the baptistery, and part of the north transept. The architects were George L. Heins and C. Grant LaFarge, and later Cram and Ferguson. Associated architects, who de-signed some of the apsidal chapels, were Henry Vaughan and Carrere and Hastings.

The first pair of architects for the cathedral planned a transitional Byzantine structure with some Romanesque aspects. Cram and Ferguson changed the design to French Gothic, necessitating alterations in the choir and sanctuary, so that these sections would match the rest of the building. The cathedral is cruciform, facing east. The core of the building is of Maine granite, the exterior walls are of Mohegan granite from Peekskill, New York, and the interior walls of Indiana limestone and Wisconsin dolomite. Two towers are planned for the west front; these will make the height of the church 267 feet. The building is over one-tenth of a mile long, and seats 8,600 people.

A cursory description of the cathedral's decoration would (and does) fill an entire book, and so will not be attempted here, except to note how readily details from medieval France or other distant times and places become American. Great truth for any single age and country is great truth for any other.

Will the cathedral ever be finished? Though unfinished, it is a fascinating sight and an expression of faith.

New York, New York

George L. Heins and C. Grant LaFarge; Cram and Ferguson; and Others, Architects

CATHEDRAL CHURCH OF ST. JOHN THE DIVINE

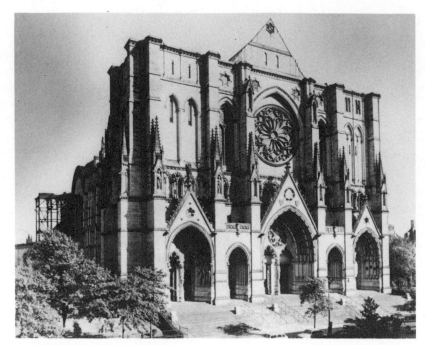

CATHEDRAL CHURCH OF ST. JOHN THE DIVINE—WEST FRONT

CATHEDRAL CHURCH OF ST. JOHN THE DIVINE—INTERIOR

First Church of Christ, Scientist
New York, New York
Carrere and Hastings, *Architects*

Gothic was not the only traditional style in which churches were built during the Gilded Age. Although the church was the only type of building for which classical was not then the leading style, still the period produced many fine classical churches. A particularly beautiful church of that style and era is the First Church of Christ, Scientist, in New York City, a structure designed by the great classical architects Carrere and Hastings.

The exterior is so massive in its plan that the building appears smaller than it is, and the steeple shorter. While the outside of the building is noble, it is within the church that the classical unleashes its full potential.

The auditorium is a masterwork. In this space, the building's largest, 1,800 people can be accommodated in the carved Circassian walnut pews on a main floor and balcony. Six magnificent chandeliers hang from the elaborately sculpted plaster ceiling. Facing the platform that holds the readers and the organ, made by Hutchings Votey and Company of Boston, is John La Farge's glowing etched glass window, *The Resurrection of Lazarus*.

Directly above the auditorium is the reading room, now the Sunday School room, which is reached by elevators. With its large skylight, handsome literature desk, and marvelous side rooms, originally used as offices for the Christian Science practitioners but now used for Sunday School classes, this area is one more instance of how well classical design can be adapted to any specialized need.

The building opened in 1903 and has been greatly prized ever since by its parishioners who—happily for lovers of architecture—continue to maintain it with care.

New York, New York   *Carrere and Hastings, Architects*
FIRST CHURCH OF CHRIST, SCIENTIST

First Church of Christ, Scientist—Auditorium

First Church of Christ, Scientist—Auditorium

First Church of Christ, Scientist—Reading Room

Unity Temple

Oak Park, Illinois

Frank Lloyd Wright, *Architect*

Frank Lloyd Wright was a competent architect. Not a great architect, by any means. But like a number of other competent, not great, artists such as Gertrude Stein and Pablo Picasso, Wright mastered the trick of fashioning products so weird, and then trumpeting about them so loud, that the public was hoodwinked into thinking that they could not understand these creations, and therefore could not judge them, but that there had to be something to warrant all the hoopla. Wright also had a complex private life; even his friend and influence, advertising man Elbert Hubbard could not have done so much for Wright's reputation as an architect as did gossip. People professionally connected with architecture, even more than the general public, are always anxious for some personal information on an architect, and architectural insiders will tout the work of its subject even if the quality of his architecture cannot match the quality of the data. Look what being murdered did for Stanford White, whose architecture is coincidentally worthy of such attention.

Unity Temple, built in 1906, has become very famous as an example of Wright's work. The building is silly, but silly enough for Wright to get away with it. It looks pretty normal to present-day eyes that have grown used to Unity Temple's even sillier descendants. It is made mainly of reinforced concrete; this fact is supposed to thrill everyone, since using this material at the time was considered innovative. Concrete is not as beautiful as limestone, and a material new to architecture does not fix up a bizarre design. The same wooden mould was used repeatedly in making the exterior walls, so that all the elevations of all sections of the building are all the same.

The church and parish house are two boxes connected with a third. The church contains a pulpit with an organ loft behind it, and pews on both the main floor and balconies. The parish house has classrooms and other chambers surrounding a center area. All decoration (such as there is) and fixtures fit the mood of the place.

Such was Wright's answer to a church on a budget. It is hard to believe, though, that a classical church and parish house could not have been built cheaper and more beautiful. And at least as functional: Wright once remarked he spent his life bruising his knees on furniture of his own design.

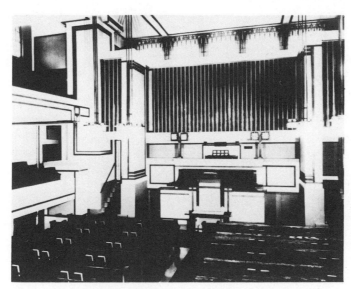

UNITY TEMPLE—CHURCH AUDITORIUM

Oak Park, Illinois   *Frank Lloyd Wright, Architect*

UNITY TEMPLE
Drawing by the architect.

FOR THE WORSHIP OF GOD
AND THE SERVICE OF MAN

Cathedral Church of St. Peter and St. Paul

Washington, District of Columbia

George Bodley and Henry Vaughan; Frohman, Robb and Little, *Architects*

The Cathedral Church of St. Peter and St. Paul is more often known as the Washington Cathedral. Although it is the cathedral of the Episcopal Diocese of Washington, it serves as the unofficial church of the country, and so is also called the National Cathedral.

Construction began in 1907, with George Bodley (of London, England) and Henry Vaughan the architects. The Bethlehem Chapel on the crypt level became in 1912 the first part of the church to be opened. After the death of the original architects, Philip Hubert Frohman, then of Frohman, Robb and Little, became the principal architect in 1921. The building is not expected to be completed before 1985.

Being built according to fourteenth-century Gothic style, the church is of Indiana limestone without steel support. Flying buttresses carry the weight of the vaulted ceiling. The plan is cruciform; above the crossing rises a central tower containing carillon and English ring. Two towers are to be added to the west front.

The decoration of the church has many references to American history, because of the cathedral's location and its sometime function.

Frohman, understanding that the great architectural styles from the past have lost none of their usefulness to the present, once said, "If we progress as a Christian civilization and if our architects prove equal to the task of expressing our loftiest aspirations, it is possible that we may even transcend the architecture of the Middle Ages."

Washington, District of Columbia   *George Bodley and Henry Vaughan; Frohman, Robb and Little, Architects*

CATHEDRAL CHURCH OF ST. PETER AND ST. PAUL

CATHEDRAL CHURCH OF ST. PETER AND ST. PAUL—THE CROSSING

]203[

CATHEDRAL CHURCH OF ST. PETER AND ST. PAUL—BETHLEHEM CHAPEL

]204[

12
Government Buildings

The buildings of the various levels of government reflect the power of the government, and, in a democracy, the power of the system. A democracy ought to build as wonderful structures as possible, since these will show the world that democracy makes the average citizen able to own, use, and enjoy great works of art.

The United States and its local divisions have long built magnificent public structures, and these have been endowed with a republican flavor. Until the present age, government buildings were usually classical, mindful not only of the style's talent at appearing imposing, when that quality is sought, but also of the nation's inheritance from Roman law, so sought by the founders of the United States.

Even through the Romantic Era, and long after modernism had become the prevalent style for most other structures, government continued to erect classical buildings. Some government buildings dating from today are classical, and some have classical notions hiding in their design. This is not due to a stick-in-the-mud aspect of government, but to this one style being the most expressive of American principles.

Other structures illustrated in this book that were built by government are libraries, museums, a school, and a bridge.

Philadelphia City Hall

Philadelphia, Pennsylvania

John McArthur, Jr., *Architect*

Although its original designs date from eleven years earlier than the usual range of this book, Philadelphia City Hall was erected from 1872 to 1901, well into the architectural Gilded Age, and serves as a fine example of government continuing to build in the classical style during a period of romantic art.

Its site selected by popular vote, the building occupies an entire public square that William Penn, the city's founder, had planned into the grid in which he laid out Philadelphia. A first story of granite supports six upper stories of brick, faced with white marble, and topped by a mansard roof. The building is a rectangle, surrounding an open courtyard, entered through archways at the bottom center of each elevation. At the north side, a tower rises to 548 feet at the top of the Penn statue. The City Hall remains the world's tallest inhabited structure without a steel skeleton, and was the world's tallest inhabited building until 1909.

The building is clad outside and in with sculpture. All the architectural sculpture was designed by Alexander Milne Calder, a Scottish immigrant and father of Alexander Stirling Calder, a sculptor represented in this volume by the Witherspoon Building; the son was in turn the father of the present-day sculptor, Alexander Calder, best known for his mobiles. The crowning bronze statue of William Penn is 37 feet tall and weighs 53,348 pounds. Also bedecking the building are sculptures of such as Indians and settlers, the seasons, the elements, the continents, virtues and vices, heroes and powers, the races of mankind, arts and sciences, trades and industries, and animals.

The interior rooms are arranged on either side of a wide corridor, on which opens every office; this is a particularly American touch, since European government buildings generally have numerous antechambers blocking people from official. Among the most impressive rooms are the two-story high Mayor's Reception Room, with blue-and-gold ceiling and red marble columns; the Conversation Hall of City Councils (now the Caucus Room), planned as five stories high but built as three stories, or a mere 55 feet; and the Supreme Court of Pennsylvania, containing bronze caryatids.

The City Hall was controversial for many years. Aside from the unsurpassed political intrigues that attended its inception and growth, a major battle from the 1920s to the 1960s raged over its architectural qualities—or lack of them. Inspired by the New Louvre of 1852–1857, the City Hall's exterior is a product of the Second Empire, which gave similar city halls (but none so grand as Philadelphia's) to cities throughout the world, including Paris. The modernists made it a special target during the years they could more easily believe their own style to be deliverance. But time has silenced such discussion, and the City Hall remains beautiful.

Philadelphia, Pennsylvania   *John McArthur, Architect*

PHILADELPHIA CITY HALL

This rendering made during construction shows building as it ultimately looked.

Pension Building
Washington, District of Columbia
Montgomery Meigs, *Architect*

The almost outrageous optimism of the Gilded Age is pointed up by the very attempt from 1882 to 1885 to construct the Pension Building in the form of no less than the Farnese Palace in Rome. Not only was insufficient money—well less than a million dollars—to be spent on the Washington structure, but also American architecture had not yet developed to the extent a close approximation would be possible. Nevertheless, the building was amazingly successful. While hardly as beautiful as Antonio da Sangallo's original, Gen. Montgomery Meigs's copy was helped by being out and out American.

The red brick building rises three stories to a cornice beneath a vast clerestory, formed by a pair of gable roofs that cross one above the other. The windows of the building's first story are square; those of the second and third stories have alternately pointed and curved pediments. Between the first and second stories, and surrounding the entire building, is a band of terra-cotta relief, three feet high and 1,200 feet long. The edifice having been built for administration of pensions to Union veterans of the Civil War or their families, the frieze depicts Union soldiers—artillery, cavalry, infantry, medical, navy, and quartermaster corps—on the move. At the bottom center of each elevation is an entrance to the building, and each of these is labeled by a plaque as Gate of the Infantry, Gate of the Invalids, Naval Gate, or Gate of the Quartermaster, and have on their spandrels figures representing Justice, Truth, War, and Wisdom. The sculpture of the frieze and the gates is the work of Casper Buberl.

The structure is practically hollow, although the large central room is isolated from the outside walls by small chambers, the upper ones being reached via the balconies. Two rows of four acanthus columns trisect the main hall, which aside from its business-as-usual function—currently the building is occupied by the Selective Service System—is ideal for presidential inaugural balls, and has been the site of a number of them.

PENSION BUILDING—INTERIOR

Washington, District of Columbia   Montgomery Meigs, *Architect*
PENSION BUILDING

Allegheny County Courthouse and Jail

Pittsburgh, Pennsylvania

Henry Hobson Richardson, *Architect*

Of course, not all government buildings erected during the Gilded Age were classical. A notable structure still built in a romantic idiom, and so a precursor to modernism, is Henry Hobson Richardson's Allegheny County Courthouse and Jail, under construction from 1884 to 1888, and one of the last works of the architect who died in 1886.

The seven-story courthouse directly joins the jail, to which was added in 1909 by F. J. Osterling. The massive granite stonework of the courthouse and jail is typical of Richardson; already the unadorned surfaces that were to plague twentieth-century modern architecture are appearing. Also typical of the architect is the Romanesque style of the building, a style Richardson did much to popularize, feeling it a return to primitive design and therefore a springboard to originality in construction. Despite its architecture being rooted in modern fallacies, the building is eminently likable. If it appears strange to present-day eyes, it also did to the eyes of its period, and indeed was meant to look strange, shock being a calculated ingredient in modernism. But the shock has become a mild bump, and the building a friendly oddity that can be readily enjoyed.

Pittsburgh, Pennsylvania   *Henry Hobson Richardson, Architect*
ALLEGHENY COUNTY COURTHOUSE AND JAIL

ALLEGHENY COUNTY COURTHOUSE AND JAIL—REAR VIEW

Rhode Island State Capitol

Providence, Rhode Island

McKim, Mead and White, *Architects*

Hope for freedom led Rhode Island to be founded and freedom is proclaimed throughout the state's dazzling white Georgian marble statehouse. The building was designed by Charles Follen McKim, of McKim, Mead and White, and constructed in 1895–1904, although it was first occupied in 1900. The style is classical, which allows wide freedom while meeting the responsibility of beautiful design.

The dome (which has been floodlighted at night since 1931) is the second largest self-supporting marble dome in the world, surpassed only by that of St. Peter's in Rome. The Providence dome is topped by a bronze statue of *Independent Man,* by George T. Brewster. The figure holds an anchor, which is the symbol of Rhode Island, and a spear.

The interior of the dome shows Roger Williams founding Providence; the scene was painted by Giorgio de Felice. A Latin inscription from Tacitus, the Roman historian, is carved around the interior of the dome; a translation of the passage is, "Rare happiness of the times when it is permitted to think as you will and speak as you think."

Providence, Rhode Island   *McKim, Mead and White, Architects*
RHODE ISLAND STATE CAPITOL

RHODE ISLAND STATE CAPITOL—INDEPENDENT MAN

New York State Supreme Court, Appellate Division, First Judicial Department

New York, New York

James Lord Brown, *Architect*

Architecture, sculpture, and mural painting were always companions until the modernists drove the first two apart and wholly disposed of the third. The beauty the three combined could achieve can be seen in the building of the First Judicial Department of the Appellate Division of the Supreme Court of New York State, a department founded in 1894 and which handles most appeal cases from Manhattan and the Bronx. The building was designed by James Lord Brown, and decorated by a host of artists. Begun in 1896 and taken possession of by the court in 1900, the building cost $633,768, a full third of which went for decoration.

Upon a basement, two stories rise to a cornice, above which is an attic topped by a balustrade. The building has two exposed elevations, one on Twenty-fifth Street and one on Madison Avenue. The Twenty-fifth Street front is the main facade, but, although of course related, the Madison Avenue side presents a facade more complete in itself than the usual end of a building.

The building is entered via a short flight of stairs at the center of the Twenty-fifth Street facade. A statue by Frederick Wellington Ruckstuhl is at each side of the staircase: *Wisdom* is at left and *Force* at right. On pedestals either behind the statues or on the stairs sit six Corinthian columns that support the entablature and the pediment. Behind the columns are two groups, *Morning and Night*, and *Noon and Evening*, by Maximilian N. Schwartzott. The pediment contains the group *Triumph of the Law*, by Charles Niehaus, and is crowned by *Justice*, with *Power* and *Study*, all three by Daniel Chester French.

Human figures symbolizing various traditions of law line the balustrade above the attic. Originally, *Mohammed*, representing Islamic law, by Charles A. Lopez, was at the far left of the facade, but the statue was removed in the mid-1950s at the request of a number of Islamic nations, since that religion forbids representation in art of human beings. All the other statues on the Twenty-fifth Street side were then moved left one position; no new statue has been added to the right. The statues remaining are, from left to right. *Zoroaster*, representing Persian law, by Edward C. Potter; *Alfred the Great*, representing Anglo-Saxon law, by J. S. Hartley; *Lycurgus*, representing Spartan law, by George E. Bissell; *Solon*, representing Athenian law, by Herbert Adams; *Saint Louis* (Louis IX), representing French law, by John Donoghue; *Manu*, representing Indian law, by Augustus Lukeman; and *Justinian*, representing Roman law, by Henry K. Bush-Brown.

On the Madison Avenue facade, four Corinthian columns rise to the entablature and cornice, upon which stand, one above each column, four caryatids depicting the seasons, by Thomas Shields Clarke. Upon the left end of the balustrade of that facade stands *Confucius*, representing Chinese law, by Philip Martiny, and upon the right, *Moses,* representing Hebraic law, by William Couper. At the center is *Peace*, by Karl Bitter.

The interior is especially notable for its mural paintings. John LaFarge was overall adviser for this type of decoration. In the entrance hall, facing the building's main door, is H. Siddons Mowbray's *Transmission of the Law*, in which is symbolized the development of the law through stages Mosaic, Egyptian, Greek, Roman, Byzantine, Norman, Common, and Modern. *Justice* is represented on both side walls, to the left by Willard L. Metcalf, and to the right by Robert Reid. The wall containing the door was painted by Reid, Metcalf, and Charles Y. Turner.

The three large murals in the courtroom are *The Justice of Law*, by Edward E. Simmons; *Wisdom*, by Henry O. Walker; and *The Power of the Law*, by Edwin H. Blashfield. The seals of the city and the state are by George W. Maynard. At the top of the opposite wall is Kenyon Cox's *The Reign of Law*. Joseph Lauber did the sixteen panels showing *Judicial and Other Virtues*. The stained glass windows and dome are by Maitland Armstrong and Company.

To the rear of the building is a six-story addition, which is classical by definition, and, of course, is undecorated, as its 1956 date would suggest.

The question present-day visitors to the main building ask themselves is, why all this beauty for a small courthouse? They ought to ask, why not all this beauty for every public building?

New York, New York   *James Lord Brown, Architect*
NEW YORK STATE SUPREME COURT, APPELLATE DIVISION,
FIRST JUDICIAL DEPARTMENT

New York City Police Headquarters
New York, New York

Hoppin and Koen, *Architects*

After Theodore Roosevelt (that symbol of the Gilded Age) had cleaned up the New York City Police Department during his reign as commissioner, it seemed natural a few years later that a new police headquarters would add to the respectability he had created. The site of the 1905–1909 building is in crowded lower Manhattan, and so tight that the lions at the front door are obliged to turn sideways, so as not to unlawfully obstruct the sidewalk. The classical style is perfect for the structure, since if only part of the building can be seen, the rich ornament of the style is sufficient to satisfy the viewer, and the regularity of classical design suggests the rest of the building.

A basement level of plain walls and rectangular windows comes above ground due to the slant of the site. The first three stories are rusticated, with arched windows on the first floor, pedimented ones on the second, and rectangular ones on the third. Above the entrance are four Corinthian columns, supporting a pediment at the attic floor, a level that contains an elaborate array of ornaments. A narrow drum supports clocks, a dome, and a cupola.

The structure will soon be superseded by a modern headquarters building, and the old edifice may be torn down. It is one of a number of wonderful buildings that can be enjoyed on a walk through New York's government district (as is the Municipal Building, which also appears in this chapter). The contrast of a walk through the modern sections of midtown Manhattan might make one wonder if the critics of the City Beautiful movement are then the proponents of a City Ugly movement.

New York, New York　　　　　　*Hoppin and Koen, Architect*

NEW YORK CITY POLICE HEADQUARTERS

Army War College

Washington, District of Columbia

McKim, Mead and White, *Architects*

The U. S. Army, noted for its matter-of-fact manner in construction, erected during 1906–1908 a matter-of-fact classical building, designed by McKim, Mead and White. Although the building almost seems to be repeated endlessly in army buildings across the country, the building certainly has considerable merit, especially if compared with the present-day army buildings that repeat across the land.

A small dome tops the center section. Two Ionic columns are found in a round arch that extends into the pediment, in which an eagle is framed. A similar arrangement is at the building's ends. A row of pilasters make up most of the walls of the wing's first two stories. The third story is recessed to support a gable roof surrounded by antefixae .

The Army War College was organized at the suggestion of Elihu Root, Secretary of War under President McKinley, for the advanced training of officers. Now the home of the interservice National War College, the building shows that through good classical design, a utilitarian building can be artistic.

Washington, D. C.   *McKim, Mead and White, Architects*
ARMY WAR COLLEGE

Manhattan Municipal Building
New York, New York

McKim, Mead and White, *Architects*

Erected in 1908 as an office building to house various city departments serving the borough, the Manhattan Municipal Building is located in that gallery of classical structures that make up the government district.

The Municipal Building is so large that Chambers Street runs through it; the concept of a road going through a building greatly appealed to the Gilded Age's love of magnitude, and is to be seen in such structures as Whitney Warren's New York Central Building (illustrated earlier in this book); McKim, Mead and White's Narragansett Casino of 1881–1884; and even in such relatively diminutive works as Peabody and Stearn's Kragsyde (also shown earlier). The intervention of the street in the Municipal Building divides the ground plan of the structure into two quadriliaterals. Over most of that area are set open vaults, access to the upper floors being gained through two entrance halls separated by Chambers Street. The massive building seldom touches the ground, but is supported by steel girders that run down into bedrock. A three-story screen crosses the facade; the screen bears three names of the island, Manhattan, New Amsterdam, and New York, and the founding dates of the last two. Behind the screen, the building rises to over 20 stories. It is topped by a tower crowned with a statue of Civic Virtue.

The very massiveness that makes the building impressive also makes it oppressive. Although all its features taken separately are fine, the building as a whole is too big and heavy. During daylight hours, the structure is simply bulky; at night, it appears downright threatening.

New York, New York   *McKim, Mead and White, Architects*

MANHATTAN MUNICIPAL BUILDING

United States Post Office, Pennsylvania Station

New York, New York

McKim, Mead and White, *Architects*

The country's most famous post office makes use of two of classical architecture's best abilities: to impress and to amuse. Its architect was William Mitchell Kendall, of McKim, Mead and White. Pennsylvania Station opened in 1914, across Eighth Avenue from the train station of the same name, and in 1918 had its use and name changed to General Post Office. In 1935, an addition opened, with which the entire structure covered two full city blocks.

The impressive Eighth Avenue facade is lined with twenty Corinthian columns behind a wide outpouring of steps. Behind every column is a pilaster, each pair of pilasters linked by a door, with pediment alternately curved or pointed, above which is a grill for light and an upper window. The pavilions bear pilasters, upper windows, and empty niches. The architect badgered each succeeding postmaster for sculpture for the niches, but was never successful in this cause. (The Ninth Avenue facade has the building's only sculpture, figures of Night and Day, signifying the postal service's working hours, which figures surround the seal of the United States; the group is by Charles Keck.) Above the colonnade and the pavilions of the Eighth Avenue facade is an attic with windows above intercolumnations and inscriptions on the pavilions. Intricate antefixae run along the attic, and the pavilions are topped by pyramids of boxes.

The talent to amuse is carried out in the building's inscriptions and decoration. The pavilions of the main facade present to Eighth Avenue and Thirty-first and Thirty-third streets inscriptions telling a brief history of the world's mail delivery. The main corridor of the post office has on its ceiling the coats of arms of ten nations of the Universal Postal Union: Belgium, Netherlands, Italy, France, England, the United States, Germany, Russia, Spain, and Austro-Hungary. By words and designs, this post office tells of all other post offices and the service they provide.

Then of course there is the famous inscription across the 280-foot frieze of the Eighth Avenue facade: NEITHER SNOW NOR RAIN NOR HEAT NOR GLOOM OF NIGHT STAYS THESE COURIERS FROM THE SWIFT COMPLETION OF THEIR APPOINTED ROUNDS. This sentence, which has become the unofficial motto of the U. S. Postal Service, is from Herodotus VIII: 98; the author's name is at the bottom far right of the frieze. The architect, who read Greek for a pastime, came across the passage one day during the period in which he designed the post office. None of the available translations were acceptable renderings, so the translation on the frieze is the architect's own.

New York, New York *McKim, Mead and White, Architects*
UNITED STATES POST OFFICE, PENNSYLVANIA STATION

San Francisco City Hall

San Francisco, California

Bakewell and Brown, *Architects*

If the San Francisco City Hall, built from 1912 to 1915, is compared with the Philadelphia City Hall, designed more than forty years earlier (and illustrated at the beginning of this chapter), the total absorption of classicism into American architecture and the full emergence of a true American classical architecture can be easily seen. The architect of the San Francisco City Hall was Arthur Brown, Jr., of Bakewell and Brown; much of the building's ornament is usually attributed to Jean-Louis Bourgeois.

Four-story wings, with two-story Roman Ionic columns forming a colonnade upon a rusticated first level, spread from the sides of the central section, which has, on each of its opposite facades, entrances on the first level supporting above an arrangement of columns that carry a sculptured pediment. Over the central section rises the most beautiful product of the long tradition of American domes.

Beneath the dome on the interior is a great hall with a magnificent cascade of stairs. The coffered curve of the dome interior is supported by a ring of composite columns and contains an oculus that reveals a second dome with trophies and the city arms.

The City Hall is placed among other marvelous buildings, including, to the west, the War Memorial Veterans Building and the War Memorial Opera House (pictured later in this volume), both structures from 1932, and both the work of Brown. Together, the three buildings surround a formal court, and form a proud achievement of American architecture.

San Francisco, California   *Bakewell and Brown, Architects*
SAN FRANCISCO CITY HALL
The ungainly pool was added in 1961 by Douglas Baylis, landscape architect, with
Wurster, Bernardi and Emmons; and Skidmore, Owings and Merrill, architects.

13
Schools and Colleges

During the Gilded Age, American education had not yet assumed the rigidity it has today. Although the national ideal of education for all was usually kept, the ideal consisted of only elementary learning, the three Rs. After this basic schooling, the child (or his circumstances) would decide between going to work, learning a craft through the apprentice system, or continuing in scholastic studies. This more flexible approach to education, having no emphasis on unnecessary degrees, provided a work force in which people would more likely find their way into jobs most suitable for them.

Higher education was given a boost by business because, as much as its self-educated moguls hated to admit it, manufacturing was becoming dependent on academically-trained scientists. But the growth of the colleges was not only for purely practical reasons; that insatiable interest in absolutely everything, a mark of the Gilded Age, brought about an increased desire for extended education. Johns Hopkins, the first modern graduate university, was founded in 1867 at the start of the Gilded Age, and by the era's end the country possessed a vast number of universities. The Gilded Age had seen the infancy of what critics called "the Ph.D. octopus," which greatly reduced in subsequent periods the diplomaless opportunity of the pre-World War I era.

The United States created buildings for its schools and colleges, public and private, with the same pride with which it built its other structures. (Along with the buildings in this chapter, educational institutions also erected the Low Library at Columbia, the Widener Library at Harvard, and the University Museum at Penn, three edifices described elsewhere in these pages.)

Alexander Hall, Princeton University
Princeton, New Jersey

William A. Potter, *Architect*

The romantic architecture of the early Gilded Age had begun to fade some years before the definite decision to turn the nation toward classical architecture was made at the Chicago 1893 World's Columbian Exposition. Right up until the fair, however, romantic buildings were still being erected in great quantity.

In 1892, Princeton University built Alexander Hall, designed by William A. Potter. The hall, which houses concerts, lectures, and other gatherings, is a work of powerful stonework in inventive shapes and arrangements. A two-story bow containing doors in Romanesque arches forms a semicircular lobby to the auditorium. A pair of towers divides the bow, while two massive towers terminate its sweep and frame a bold facade of sculpture by J. Massey Rhind and large, round windows beneath a gabled roof. The auditorium holds pews on the main floor and the balcony, facing a curious stage bearing inlay.

For all its wayward design, Alexander Hall is very imposing, far more so than its close relative (illustrated in the previous chapter), Richardson's

ALEXANDER HALL, PRINCETON UNIVERSITY—INTERIOR

Allegheny County Courthouse and Jail, even though the function of Richardson's building is more imposing than that of Potter's. It is the setting that makes the difference; the city needs formal design, while in the countryside, where the town of Princeton still remains, there is a place for picturesque romantic architecture.

Princeton, New Jersey   *William A. Potter, Architect*

ALEXANDER HALL, PRINCETON UNIVERSITY

Campus Plan, Columbia University
New York, New York
McKim, Mead and White, *Planners*

Not only individual buildings, but also their arrangement among each other and their landscaping ought to be beautiful; this was the credo of the City Beautiful movement, that concept so derided in the present age when architects openly state their dread of both the city and beauty. A City Beautiful plan in miniature within New York, a city which, early imprinted with a stark grid plan, has little opportunity for grand arrangement, is the present site of Columbia University. When it was decided to move the college to Morningside Heights from the area around Madison Avenue and Forty-ninth Street, a competition was held for the best design of a campus with boundaries of Broadway, Amsterdam Avenue, 120th, and 116th streets; the final plan

extended to 114th Street. The winners of the competition were McKim, Mead and White.

To create in a busy city an atmosphere of contemplation, the designers enclosed most of the plan within a wall of buildings, and arranged the inside buildings to enclose open areas that seem separate from the city's activity. These open areas are resplendent with walks and terraces, fountains and statues that form an integral part of City Beautiful design. The most impressive vista in the final plan is between buildings A (the Low Library, illustrated later in this book) and CC. The entire campus plan is symmetrical, which ties every part of the design to its opposite part and therefore unifies the design.

Columbia today retains a coherent campus in the middle of a city that would have swallowed up a much larger campus of less rigid design. And it is a beautiful campus. It demonstrates not only how a college would appear in the City Beautiful, but also gives an idea how the City Beautiful itself would appear.

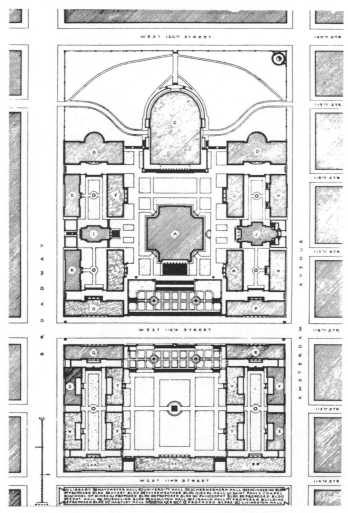

New York, New York   *McKim, Mead and White, Architects*
CAMPUS PLAN, COLUMBIA UNIVERSITY

Men's Dormitories University of Pennsylvania

Philadelphia, Pennsylvania

Cope and Stewardson, *Architects*

The growth of higher education during the Gilded Age, and that period's longing for Old World culture, brought to many American colleges the look of venerable English universities. A fine product of this trend is the University of Pennsylvania's Men's Dormitories (now called, in honor of coeducation, the University Quadrangle), designed by Cope and Stewardson and built from 1895 to 1910 with later additions. Covering a vast area and enclosing large fields, the dorms sleep 1,500.

The style is Elizabethan-Jacobean. Such correct adaptations as these dormitories, Trumbauer's Gothic buildings at Duke University, and Cram's dormitories, also Gothic, at Princeton, are not archaeological reproductions of foreign structures, but are buildings in traditional styles, styles alive and by their nature international, styles that have evolved to a state fitting for each building's soil and date.

Philadelphia, Pennsylvania   *Cope and Stewardson, Architects*
MEN'S DORMITORIES, UNIVERSITY OF PENNSYLVANIA

Colt Memorial High School

Bristol, Rhode Island

Cooper and Bailey, *Architects*

The Gilded Age was a time when beauty was a quality as naturally to be desired in architecture as a roof. So it is that the small town of Bristol, Rhode Island, has a high school that has never ceased to draw gawking admirers.

Built in 1906 from the designs of Cooper and Bailey, the building is of white Georgian marble, offset with bronze decorations. At each side of the front door are a pair of Corinthian columns beneath a pediment that bears sculpture. At each end of the structure's front section, which carries a hip roof, is a lesser arrangement of a pair of columns separated by the door. The windows occur in groups, each group surrounded by a single moulding. A wing at the back of the building houses solely the school auditorium.

Today, of course, such a noble design would never be considered for a school. Not only is the classical style out of fashion, but the children—whether from city slums or the best suburban homes—would naturally be expected to deface any high school no end, making such elegance not worth the slight extra expenses it costs to achieve. Yet the Bristol children do not deface their high school. Could it not be that they realize such grandeur was built for them, and that the building shows that their elders think of them as more than vandals to be contained, and that this opinion of themselves restrains ideas of destruction?

Bristol, Rhode Island   *Cooper and Bailey, Architects*

COLT MEMORIAL HIGH SCHOOL

Maclaurin Buildings, Massachusetts Institute of Technology

Cambridge, Massachusetts

Welles Bosworth, *Architect*

A spectacular vision is found at the Massachusetts Institute of Technology, where a number of buildings are joined together around three sides of an open area to form the Grand Court. The open end of the court faces the Charles River directly. Closing the top of the court are the Maclaurin Buildings. Actually a single structure, the building, whose function has always been instructional, was begun in 1913, dedicated in 1916, and named after Richard Cockburn Maclaurin, president of the institute from 1909 to 1920. The architect was Welles Bosworth, M. I. T. '89.

Ten Ionic columns cross the front of the center section, and support an entablature bearing the school's name. The nearly undecorated attic and dome, as well as the plain wings, let the building take its beauty from its classical shapes.

The dependence on shape, the sparsity of decoration, and the wall of glass behind the columns might be seen as anticipating modern design. But Bosworth, always a traditional architect, was showing another—and very fine—side of the classical. The stark modern building is not a descendant of this structure, since this building boasts a classical design, emphasizing one aspect of it more than another.

Cambridge, Massachusetts   *Welles Bosworth, Architect*
MACLAURIN BUILDINGS, MASSACHUSETT: INSTITUTE OF TECHNOLOGY

MACLAURIN BUILDINGS, MASSACHUSETTS INSTITUTE OF TECHNOLOGY—
COLUMNS AND GLASS WALL

American Academy in Rome
Rome, Italy
McKim, Mead and White, *Architects*

One of the reasons present-day architecture is so bad is the lack of training given architectural students today. Four years of general undergraduate studies are prerequisite for three years of postgraduate work more specifically in architecture. Seven years would seem to be more than sufficient, but a close examination of what is actually taught during that time would prove the training to be more time-consuming than instructional.

The university course in architecture is set up similarly to every other course, which means the student has very few hours per week in the class-room. While this arrangement might lend itself to the study of, say, Latin, where much time in private is required for reading and translation, the practical study of architecture needs extensive work under the eye of the teacher. Since so little classroom time is available, the students are told to practice the Modern virtue of "originality" and to let the design spring from the mind. The schools attempt to fill the gaps in architectural training with courses in such supposedly-related subjects as sociology and psychology. Little wonder it is a common occurrence today for architectural firms to hire a young person just out of school, a student who comes recommended by his professors and with a record of top grades, only to discover he actually has no idea of how to build a real building.

During the Gilded Age, the training of American architects was more practical. A number of young men attended the École des Beaux Arts in Paris, which had no equal anywhere in the world. The school was dedicated to teaching classical art, although the École also espoused rationalism (now called functionalism) ; this preaching of modern theory should be remembered by modernists who deprecatingly use the words "Beaux Arts" to symbolize all they consider wrong in the classical architecture of the Gilded Age. At the École the students worked mainly in ateliers, small groups headed by established architects. The work of each student was carefully inspected by both the leader of the atelier and the other students. The study was long, difficult, and intense, but it gave the young architects a thorough knowledge of the profession.

Rome, Italy　　　　　　　　　　　　*McKim, Mead and White, Architects*
AMERICAN ACADEMY IN ROME

Many more American Gilded Age architects were trained in leading American architectural firms. Richard Morris Hunt, who had been a student at the École, set up his own atelier in New York City; the New York firm of McKim, Mead and White was later considered the best native training ground for American architects. As American architectural firms imitated the French ateliers, so was established the American Academy in Rome, which imitated the French Academy that was housed in the Villa Medici there. As the French government gave the Prix de Rome, a scholarship to French nationals to study in that classical city, so private Americans gave the Rome Prize to citizens of the United States. The American Academy was organized by such architects as Charles Follen McKim and Thomas Hastings; the financing was in large part from J. P. Morgan.

The American Academy in Rome was housed in an American structure built in 1913 after the designs of McKim, Mead and White; the edifice is perfectly suited to its foreign location. Beneath a slanting roof, five pairs of windows, a small window above a large, are separated and surrounded by single composite pilasters. Five round arches line the rusticated first story, which is reached by a large flight of stairs. Pavilions at both sides of the central facade each surround their own court, which opens off the larger court that is bound by an ornate gate. The interiors are restrained and dignified. A special feature is the court, with fountain, at the building's center.

The American Academy in Rome continues to operate, although it obviously seeks little influence on American architecture today. The Rome Prize is still given, but the French government has discontinued sponsoring the Prix de Rome, because, in the words of André Malraux, Minister of Cultural Affairs, "Rome has nothing basic to teach architects."

AMERICAN ACADEMY IN ROME—LIBRARY

AMERICAN ACADEMY IN ROME—COURTYARD

14
Libraries

Every stratum of Gilded Age life saw the library differently. To the millionaire collector, the library was the room or even separate building that had to be made artistically suitable to hold the marvelous books he considered as worthy of being collected as paintings and bronzes. The intellectual viewed the university or public library as he does today, although with greater optimism; he more often sought there knowledge not only for its own sake and for developing his own character, but also for improving the world's future.

To the average citizen, the library appeared a way to better his station. Business had not yet become degree-conscious, and the man who simply knew his field had as much chance of getting ahead as did the man who had a diploma that might prove his knowledge. Millions did indeed struggle in libraries for personal improvement, cultural as well as monetary. Thomas Edison, whose formal education had taken three months, worked in his teens as a candy butcher on the daily train between Detroit and his home of Port Huron, so that during the day he could study in the larger city's library. The self-help, rags-to-riches potential of such efforts appealed to the wealthy, who had often gone the same course, and libraries became a favorite benefaction of the millionaires, especially of one.

With the great importance that all segments of the people attached to libraries, it is little wonder they were housed in some of the most spectacular buildings of an age of spectacular buildings.

Library of Congress
Washington, District of Columbia
Smithmeyer and Pelz, *Architects*

An Act of Congress in 1800 created the Library of Congress as a reference library for legislators. When the Capitol was set afire in 1814, the original collection was destroyed, leading Thomas Jefferson to sell the extensive contents of his personal library to the government at cost. Today the facility serves also as a national library, and has probably the largest collection of any library in the world.

The present home of the library was built from 1886 to 1897, from Smithmeyer and Pelz's designs that were based on the Paris Opera House. As originally built, the library was in the shape of an open rectangle with inside sections between the centers of opposite sides and with a dome at the crossing. The longer facades have massive center sections, reflected in the smaller corner pavilions. All around the exterior, a rustic base supports a short first story, that can be entered by way of a grand staircase under which vehicles can pass. A taller second story bears columns on center sections and pavilions, both types of features having low attics.

The most impressive interior of the building is the main reading room, which occupies the entire rotunda. Ever since the Capitol was erected, Americans have felt especially drawn to a dome topping a drum; in the library's case, an octagonal drum. The rotunda, including that of the Library of Congress, reminds them of the Roman heritage in their law and architecture.

Washington, District of Columbia   Smithmeyer and Pelz, *Architects*
LIBRARY OF CONGRESS

LIBRARY OF CONGRESS—READING ROOM

Boston Public Library

Boston, Massachusetts

McKim, Mead and White, *Architects*

Casting aside the up-to-the-minute originality then (and now) fashionable that produced Richardson's peculiar Trinity Church, Charles Follen McKim, in designing the Boston Public Library that faces the church across Copley Square, had the daring originality to build in the timeless classical tradition, using the Italian Renaissance style to produce an original American building that heralded a classical era.

The imposing facade that so greatly ages the opposing Trinity Church of only ten years earlier, has as its main features a three-arched entrance with five square windows on each side of the first story, and thirteen long, arched windows on the second, surmounted by a sloping red tile roof with green copper trim. In the spandrels of the arched windows are the colophons of early printers and booksellers; these medallions are the work of Domingo Mora. Beneath each of the three center second-story windows is a panel by Augustus St. Gaudens, showing, variously, the seals of Massachusetts, the Library, and Boston; the other arched windows have beneath them the names of famous historical figures. Mora and St. Gaudens carved on the keystone of the central entrance arch the head of Minerva, goddess of wisdom. Four dramatic wrought-iron candelabra of six lanterns each surround and separate the three arches of the entrance. Immediately in front of the building, on opposite sides of the entranceway, sit large bronze sculptures, representing Art and Science, by Bela Pratt.

Behind the main entrance is a vestibule of pink Knoxville marble. Three pairs of bronze doors by Daniel Chester French depict, left doors to right, Music and Poetry, Knowledge and Wisdom, and Truth and Romance. Beyond these doors is the Roman entrance hall. A vaulted, mosaic ceiling rests on Iowa sandstone piers. On the ceiling and the white Georgian marble floor can be seen the names of people prominent in the early library and other eminent Bostonians. The handsome staircase has Siena marble walls and gray Echaillon marble steps.

The vast main reading room rises 50 feet to its barrel-vaulted ceiling. Other impressive rooms include the Puvis de Chavannes Gallery, the Abbey Room, the Elliott Room, and the Sargent Gallery, these named for the artists whose murals decorate the walls.

A splendid courtyard is at the building's center, showing grace and relaxation to most visitors, and wasted space to modern architects. An arcaded promenade, based on the Cancelleria Palace in Rome, runs along three sides of the courtyard.

In 1969–1972, a boring modern addition, designed by Philip Johnson, was built at the rear of McKim's structure. However, the newer work is sufficiently separate as not to interfere all that much with the 1888 masterpiece.

BOSTON PUBLIC LIBRARY—LANTERNS AT ENTRANCE

Boston, Massachusetts   *McKim, Mead and White, Architects*
BOSTON PUBLIC LIBRARY

BOSTON PUBLIC LIBRARY—BATES HALL (MAIN READING ROOM)

BOSTON PUBLIC LIBRARY—COURTYARD

Carnegie Free Library

Braddock, Pennsylvania

William Halsey Wood, *Architect*

Of all Andrew Carnegie's many philanthropies, his libraries are best known, and possibly the gifts he best liked making. His impoverished family had emigrated from Scotland when he was 12, and Carnegie lost no time in developing the love for the United States and its capitalistic system that he had for the rest of his life. At the turn of the century, he sold his steel business, which then became U. S. Steel, its former owner becoming, as J. P. Morgan called him, "the richest man in the world." Carnegie had gotten out of the steel business that he might get into the business of giving away just about all his money. "The man who dies thus rich, dies disgraced," he wrote. The tycoon who so favored the ladder of success that he favored a one-hundred-percent in-

heritance tax, and who himself wrote impressive literary works, came upon libraries as ideal donations that would give education and enlightenment.

The first of these libraries was in Braddock, a Pennsylvania town near Pittsburgh. The original stone building, erected in 1888–1889 and added to in 1893, continues to serve its purpose today. Designed by William Halsey Wood in the Romanesque style of the day, it is an example of an average public building then still built along romantic lines.

Carnegie was to go on to spend over 43 million dollars on the construction of public libraries. These were scattered through an astonishing number of communities, large and small, in Britain and the United States, and can be readily seen today. At first, the design of the structures was left up to the municipalities, but later contributions were usually accompanied by plans in "Carnegie Classical," usually bearing above the entrance the rays of sunrise and the motto, "LET THERE BE LIGHT."

Braddock, Pennsylvania   *William Halsey Wood, Architect*
CARNEGIE FREE LIBRARY

TWO UNIVERSITY LIBRARIES

Low Library, Columbia University
New York, New York
McKim, Mead and White, *Architects*

At the center of the plan (illustrated earlier herein) of the new Columbia University that McKim, Mead and White devised during the 1890s, stands Charles Follen McKim's Low Library, which is the center of the university's intellectual life.

A magnificent plaza precedes the main facade of ten Ionic columns supporting an attic. The building is cruciform, with a huge dome at its center.

How could a building be more direct? The force of its shape would be sufficient to satisfy the modernist love of building blocks, but yet the structure is rich enough in ornament, such as the antefixae, to satisfy the human thirst for beauty.

New York, New York   *McKim, Mead and White, Architects*
LOW LIBRARY, COLUMBIA UNIVERSITY

Harry Elkins Widener Memorial, Harvard University

Cambridge, Massachusetts

Horace Trumbauer, *Architect*

Harvard, the greatest of American universities, fittingly has the largest collection for research of any university library in the country, a research collection second in size in the United States only to that of the Library of Congress, with that of the New York Public Library coming in third. (The main buildings of both these other libraries are included in this chapter.) The vast structure that houses the Harvard collection is the Harry Elkins Widener Memorial Library, named for the young bibliophile who died upon the *Titanic* and given by his mother, Mrs. George D. Widener, who was widowed in the same disaster. The building was erected in 1912–1914, with alterations in 1938; the library's design was by the family's court architect, Horace Trumbauer.

A vast flight of stairs leads past the above-ground basement to a long row of Corinthian columns; they screen the first two stories, which are of brick, and support the brick attic.

The building is especially notable for its efficient design; at the time of its construction, it was considered the last word in library planning. Function was admirably served, and there was no need to sacrifice form.

Cambridge, Massachusetts   *Horace Trumbauer, Architect*
HARRY ELKINS WIDENER MEMORIAL LIBRARY, HARVARD UNIVERSITY

Pierpont Morgan Library

New York, New York

McKim, Mead and White, *Architects*

The American Gilded Age often is also called the American Renaissance. The period has been claimed to be the last flowering of the same Renaissance that first appeared in Italy, and there are striking similarities between, for example, the Florence of the Renaissance and the New York of the Gilded Age, such as the aristocrats emblazoned on a democratic field, the optimism, the humanism, and certainly the architecture, since much Gilded Age architecture was willfully adapted from that of the Renaissance. Of all Gilded Age personalities, the one that most clearly can be matched with a Renaissance personality is J. P. Morgan, who shared many characteristics with Lorenzo il Magnifico: both were made rich by banking, both were great collectors of antiquities, both were patrons of living artists and architects. The banker Morgan, who was an avid collector of books (as well as of many other things), hired Charles Follen McKim to design an entire building to house the book collection, and McKim, naturally enough, produced a library that is both Renaissance and American.

Completed in 1906, the library stands behind the Morgan mansion at Thirty-sixth Street and Madison Avenue. The library was presented to the public in 1924, eleven years after Morgan's death; his mansion was demolished to make way for a library addition, built in 1928 from the designs of Benjamin Wistar Morris. The original library consisted mainly of three rooms, being a reception room at the center, a bookstack room to the east, and a reading room to the west.

The rooms are housed in a rectangular marble building. A beautiful grillwork fence separates Thirty-sixth Street from the austere facade. At the facade's entrance is a recessed portico holding two pair of Ionic columns beneath a round arch. Surrounding the steps leading to the entrance are two lions by E. C. Potter; the excellence of these led to his commission to carve the famed lions at the New York Public Library. The intensity of Andrew O'Connor's carving for the facade counters the relative sparseness of sculptural decoration.

The interiors have a special place in the history of American interior decoration. Gilded Age interiors were often glorious, but the Morgan Library interiors go a step further. Superlatives ought to be sparingly used in the history of art, but it may be ventured to say the building's interiors are the best the Gilded Age produced for a building of any use.

The resplendent reception room, with its marble floors, has elegant inlay panels of gray with white border designs, which separate the marble composite columns and pilasters. The ceiling was decorated by Harry Siddons Mowbray. Along with his frescoes, illuminated in gold, of the Arthur legends, the Divine Comedy, Epic Poetry, and Lyric Poetry, he provided a lavish apex of relief figures on a blue background, the figures having been derived from classical literature.

Mowbray also decorated the ceiling of the East Room, that contains the bookstacks. Represented there are nine historical figures, and an equal number of disciplines. Beneath are three tiers of stacks, the upper two reached by balconies attained through a secret door in the lowest tier. The sixteenth-century Flemish tapestry, *The Triumph of Avarice,* and the fireplace beneath it, relieve the flow of the grill-enclosed shelves.

The finest room—breathtaking!—of the three is the West Room, the reading room. A low bookcase, also faced with grill, encircles the room; the walls above are covered with red damask. Beneath the polychrome wood ceiling, which is possibly from Cardinal Gigli's palace at Lucca, Morgan's magnificent desk faces the fireplace, attributed to Desiderio da Settignano, that stands beneath the banker's portrait by Frank Holl.

The rare books and art objects do not stand out amid the library's interiors, but seem a part of them. This is so because the interiors are a setting equal to the contents. The building is a product of twentieth-century America, and proves the art of the distant past can be rivaled today, if there is the desire to do it.

New York, New York   *McKim, Mead and White, Architects*
PIERPONT MORGAN LIBRARY

PIERPONT MORGAN LIBRARY—RECEPTION ROOM

PIERPONT MORGAN LIBRARY—EAST ROOM

PIERPONT MORGAN LIBRARY—WEST ROOM

New York Public Library, Central Building

New York, New York

Carrere and Hastings, *Architects*

"Form follows function": architects of other than the present age would laugh at the importance the modernists find in this credo. Form has always followed function, since the first roof slanted to let off the rain. The modern architect has extended the alliterative adage to the bankrupt view that man is entitled in his surroundings to nothing more than the bare necessities. A structure such as the central building of the New York Public Library certainly derives its basic shape from its use, but its architects, Carrere and Hastings, were generous enough to also endow the building with design principles that the centuries had proved beautiful.

Built on the former site of the Croton Reservoir, the library was opened on 23 May 1911 after nine years of construction. Mainly of Vermont marble, the structure is classical. The library can be entered either at the basement level on the Forty-second Street side, or at the first floor through a grand lobby at the Fifth Avenue side. Offices and specialized collections are kept throughout the building, with the main reading room and catalogue on the top floor, which is the third. Works of art decorate the building, including busts of the two architects.

Viewed from above, the effects of the function of the building on its form can be easily seen. The long reading room at the rear, covering practically the entire 390 feet of the structure's width, is clearly delineated, as is the catalogue room, perpendicularly adjoining the reading room at the center. Two wells of about 80 feet by 80 feet admit light to the rooms with windows on the inside walls. The functional long windows seen at the rear of the walls illuminate the bookstacks beneath the reading room.

But viewed from the sidewalk, the human level, the features designed to satisfy the human eye are more important than the building's well-planned functional aspects. The rectangular main entrance is divided in three by pairs of Corinthian columns and surrounded by single columns inside extending walls. A figure is above each column, separated from it by the entablature. The gable roof of the catalogue room forms a recessed pediment. On the facade wings, vertical pairs of windows—the top one square, the bottom one arched—are separated from other pairs by Corinthian columns. At each end of the facade is a porch with two columns between the walls and with an entablature that includes a pediment. At the main entrance, the two pink Tennessee marble lions by E. C. Potter look out haughtily at New York's growing number of modern buildings, no more functional, but of far less beautiful form.

NEW YORK PUBLIC LIBRARY, CENTRAL BUILDING—MAIN READING ROOM

New York, New York   *Carrere and Hastings, Architects*
NEW YORK PUBLIC LIBRARY, CENTRAL BUILDING

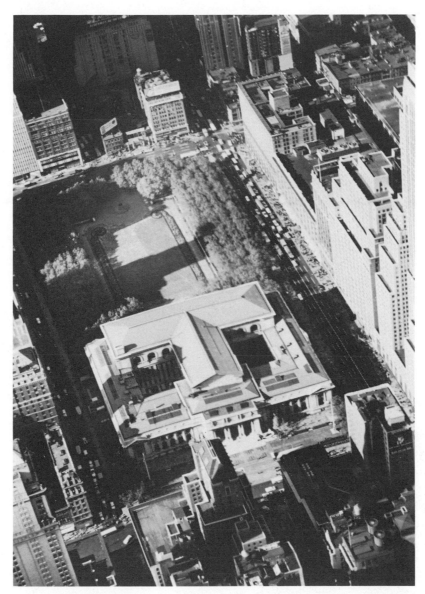

New York Public Library, Central Building—Aerial View

15
Museums

*O*n display at museums during the Gilded Age
was a nation interested in everything. This
thirst for knowledge that marks the period was evident in the success of the world's fairs held in the
United States, and spilled over into the many permanent museums, botanical gardens, and zoos that
the age built.

Displays were generally less rigorous than those
of today. The people of the Gilded Age had interests
less sophisticated and specialized (or, possibly to
put it another way, less jaded and narrow) than have
people today. A rare plant could therefore be displayed as a curiosity rather than a part of the balance
of nature, although the Gilded Age certainly produced men who would understand the plant in its
larger framework.

The art museum was then a very different concept than it is today. The great art collections were
still in the homes of the millionaires, and had not
yet been given to the museums. The Gilded Age
museum had fewer priceless treasures to show, and
instead contained exhibits designed to instill culture
in the citizenry. The displays included recent paintings, all preferably uplifting morally, and copies of
famous European sculpture, since the average American, less travelled than today, would never see the
real thing.

The country's best art museum buildings were
erected during the period between the end of the
Gilded Age and the triumph of modernism. The art
museums from this intermediate period, through
which the tradition of Gilded Age architecture still
continued, are spectacular settings for the great
contents just then acquired from the wealthy. The
best of these museums is Horace Trumbauer's
Philadelphia Museum of Art, built from 1919 to
1931; another fine structure is John Russell Pope's
1938 National Gallery of Art in Washington, a
building illustrated in the last chapter of this book.
Modern architecture, with its lack of confidence,
builds bland museums of art, excusing their ineffica-
ciousness by saying they are designed to focus all the
attention on the work of art. The Gilded Age
museum is usually rather pompous, like the culture
it wanted to distribute. But still, many are very
gallant, and, it goes without saying, better than they
would be if they were built today.

Museum Building, Smithsonian Institution
Washington, District of Columbia
Cluss and Schulze, *Architects*

After the Centennial Exposition at Philadelphia, most of the exhibits of foreign nations eventually were given to the Smithsonian Institution in Washington, increasing the size of that organization's collection four hundred percent, and necessitating a new building. The Washington architectural firm of Cluss and Schulze drew the final plans, based on earlier drawings by General Montgomery Meigs, architect of the Pension Building, which is shown earlier in these pages. The structure, today called the Arts and Industries Building, was erected 1879–1881; the total cost was $315,400 or less than three dollars per square foot—proportionately the cheapest permanent building ever built by the U. S. Government.

The Romanesque structure is square, each facade consisting of a central section with a pair of towers, and wings terminating in lanterned pavilions. The entire two and one-quarter acres of the building is roofed. A rotunda at the building's center rises 108 feet to the top of the finial.

The economy in building proved to be false. Poor construction of the roof made need for extensive repairs. Lack of sufficient basement area provided too little storage space, and the coldness of wood floors over cellarless areas caused severe illness during the 1880s among the employees, ten of whom died.

The new building was, nevertheless, the most up-to-date museum building in the country. Its displays provided for a time a continuation of the Centennial, which was so representative of its era, and today the structure gives a glimpse of the architectural style of that fair.

Washington, District of Columbia   *Cluss and Schulze, Architects*
MUSEUM BUILDING, SMITHSONIAN INSTITUTION

MUSEUM BUILDING, SMITHSONIAN INSTITUTION—ROTUNDA

University Museum, University of Pennsylvania

Philadelphia, Pennsylvania

Cope and Stewardson, *Architects;*
Wilson Eyre, Jr. and Frank Miles Day,
Associated Architects

The University of Pennsylvania's University Museum, from its inception one of the leading archaeological museums in the world, is housed in a building reflective of the passion for the exotic East that swept the Gilded Age. In fact, the very founding in 1887 of an archaeological museum was a product of that era's interest in every sort of culture.

The Gilded Age continued the fascination that earlier American eras had had with the classical cultures of Greece and Rome, and, more than previous eras, it thirsted after European civilization.

But explorations were bringing additional cultures to the attention of the Gilded Age mind, always anxious to learn. Egypt was, as it is today, instantly associated with archaeology, and its pyramids were seen on numerous stereopticon slides. Babylon and the Holy Land drew minds reared on the Bible. But China and recently-opened Japan held the greatest mystery for America and all the West, and the entire Gilded Age was influenced through and through by the East.

The romantic architects, and their descendants in the Gilded Age, were seekers after originality, and saw in Eastern architecture something new to try, even though these designs new in the West were ancient in the East. The *japonais* trend in Western art is, however, as a whole too sweeping to be regarded as merely a novelty, and must be admired for its delicacy and simplicity. The University Museum owes its design more to artistic concern with the East, the Gilded Age's interest in Eastern exoticism,

Philadelphia, Pennsylvania

Cope and Stewardson, Architects;
Wilson Eyre, Jr. and Frank Miles
Day, Associated Architects

UNIVERSITY MUSEUM, UNIVERSITY OF PENNSYLVANIA

and the appropriateness of building an archaeological museum in a style derived from a distant culture, than the romantic notions still current when the building was begun.

Construction lasted from 1893 to 1910. The architects were Cope and Stewardson, with Wilson Eyre, Jr., and Frank Miles Day associated. An addition was made in 1970 from the designs of Mitchell and Giurgola.

The main entrance is reached through an impressive courtyard, raised from the street level. The vast rotunda is typical of the Gilded Age's ability for adapting the styles of other cultures, and creating strictly American results. It is seen elsewhere in this book that the rotunda is a very American architectural element, and the rotunda of the University Museum, for all the influence of the East, could belong in no other country but the United States.

UNIVERSITY MUSEUM, UNIVERSITY OF PENNSYLVANIA—BAUGH PAVILION

Metropolitan Museum of Art

New York, New York

Richard Morris Hunt, and Others, *Architects*

The present Metropolitan Museum of Art was built on what had been unfinished ground in Central Park, and the building has been further and further encroaching on the park ever since. The park's designers, Frederick Law Olmsted and Calvert Vaux, envisioned a small museum, not nearly the size of the structure's central section, designed by Richard Morris Hunt and Richard Howland Hunt in 1894. Soon the wings were added by Hunt and Hunt, the firm of the sons of Richard Morris Hunt, who had died in 1895. Shortly following the construction of the wings, the pavilions at the wing's ends were built from the designs of McKim, Mead and White. Additions were made right up to recent date, and would continue to be made if museum officials had their way in the matter. While the grand edifice should have been built on land other than that of the crowded city's precious park, the design of the structure is nevertheless first rate.

The central facade contains four pairs of Corinthian columns surrounding three bays with rounded arches. The bays hold two small columns and a rusticated wall beneath an entablature and large window. Above each pair of large columns is the stone for trophies that were never carved. What present-day curator would waste his budget on finishing such old-fashioned foolishness, and, besides, does not the outcropping give the building a "natural" look? The attic is crowned with antefixae connected by swags. At the sides of the central facade are lower walls, each bearing three pedimented windows and two sculptures. Karl Bitter designed the central section's sculptural ornament. The wings extend beneath ridged roofs; tall arched windows line the wings, as do square windows in the lower rusticated level. Each pavilion at the end of its wing reprises the large Corinthian columns of the central facade and has a hipped roof.

During 1970, the modernists added a fantastically inappropriate mound of stairs and a pair of funny fountains. These designs show why the modernists have such contempt for American classical architecture: they cannot even understand it.

New York, New York　　　　*Richard Morris Hunt, and Others, Architects*

METROPOLITAN MUSEUM OF ART

St. Louis Museum of Art

St. Louis, Missouri

Cass Gilbert, *Architect*

The Louisiana Purchase Exposition was held at St. Louis in 1904, a century after the fact. The only permanent structure built for that noble member of the long line of marvelous world's fairs held during the Gilded Age was the central pavilion of the Palace of Art. After Forest Park had been cleared of the temporary wonders, the city was presented with the building in 1906, and the Art Museum became a successor to the St. Louis Museum of Fine Arts founded by Washington University in 1879, the oldest art museum west of the Mississippi.

Cass Gilbert was the architect for the building, which is of mainly brick and Bedford gray limestone.

Six Corinthian columns support an entablature that bears, one above each column, six statues representing periods of art: Classic, Gothic, Oriental, Egyptian, Renaissance, and Modern. Three panels by Hermon A. MacNeil, called *Ars Artium Omnium* (*The Art of All Arts*) are behind the columns; the two statues to the sides of the entrance are, west, *Sculpture* by Daniel Chester French, and, east *Painting* by Louis St. Gaudens. At the ends of the wings, which extend east and west, are pavilions with Ionic columns beneath entablatures. Also illustrated here is Sculpture Hall, which is the great central gallery of the building.

The St. Louis Museum is only one example of the fine permanent buildings that the world's fairs of the Gilded Age bequeathed to the people, along with memories of plaster grandeur.

ST. LOUIS MUSEUM OF ART—SCULPTURE HALL

St. Louis, Missouri   *Cass Gilbert, Architect*

ST. LOUIS MUSEUM OF ART

Museum of Fine Arts

Boston, Massachusetts

Guy Lowell, *Architect*

Although it contains one of the finest collections in America, the Museum of Fine Arts in Boston is not one of the Gilded Age's most beautiful art museum buildings. The structure nevertheless demonstrates how effective even a mediocre classical design can be.

Above the main entrance are four Ionic columns, with the capitals of the outer columns needlessly distorted. The pediment is too squat, but does bear handsome acroteria. Facing the Fenway, the extensive park designed by Olmsted, is a long row of Ionic columns, a facade impressive almost only because of the size and number of the columns.

But if anyone doubts the supremacy of a bland classical building over a bland modern one, let him compare, in the photograph shown here, the old building, erected 1907–1909 from the designs of Guy Lowell, to the addition of 1970–1971, for which the architects were Hugh Stubbins and Associates. Although there are ancient precedents for the old wing illustrated here, the building would be much improved by a row of upper-story windows (even false ones), instead of a blank wall. The missing second-story windows are to be found on the new addition, though now the first-story windows are gone, and the total lack of ornament makes the new structure so dull that even the awkward old wing is more satisfying. It would be better to continue the decorations, however modest, of the old section onto the new, but, then, such decoration has no function other than enhancing the appearance of the building.

Boston, Massachusetts   *Guy Lowell, Architect*
MUSEUM OF FINE ARTS

MUSEUM OF FINE ARTS, BOSTON—MAIN ENTRANCE

MUSEUM OF FINE ARTS—OLD AND NEW WINGS

Minneapolis Institute of Arts

Minneapolis, Minnesota

McKim, Mead and White, *Architects*

Cosmopolitanism was one of the great desires of the Gilded Age; the Midwest, being the most lacking in it, sought it the hardest. In 1911, the Minneapolis Society of Fine Arts owned a grand total of nine paintings, yet, from 1912 to 1915, the Society built a $520,000 museum designed by the firm of McKim, Mead and White.

The building is the classical style reduced to its plainest; this is not a criticism, since barren classical can be strikingly beautiful. The central facade con-sists of many steps before six Ionic columns which support an unembellished entablature and pediment. Each of the wings stands on a rusticated base with square windows, and contains rectangular windows separated from one another by pilasters.

However strange it would seem in the present to build such a big museum for such a small collection, the Gilded Age was a time of growth and of taking risks. The chance paid off: Minneapolis got a land-mark, the collection grew so fast that a new wing extending back from the rear of the center section was opened in 1927, a new extension is being added today by architect Kenzo Tange, and the museum now houses a large and important collection.

Minneapolis, Minnesota   *McKim, Mead and White, Architects*
MINNEAPOLIS INSTITUTE OF ARTS

16
Auditoriums and Arenas

*P*artly through necessity but mainly through desire, the Gilded Age was an era of social gathering. Theater, concerts, lectures, athletic events, and so on, could, before film and electronic entertainment, be attended only in person. Still, the Gilded Age gave special importance to going to these live activities. In those optimistic times, people wanted people as part of their lives. The period's cultural aspirations, endless interest in everything, and general joie de vivre *combined with this gregariousness to make theatres, concert and lecture halls, sports arenas, and the like, central to the leisure time of the era's inhabitants.*

Carnegie Hall
New York, New York
William Burnet Tuthill, *Architect*

Carnegie Hall was not strictly one of Andrew Carnegie's philanthropic gifts, but a commercial venture he financed. He had wanted to call it simply The Music Hall, but foreign artists refused to perform in a place whose name had its London connotation, and so the name was changed, and, as it happened, without Carnegie's knowledge. The hall dates from 1891, and was designed by William Burnet Tuthill, with Adler and Sullivan, and others, associated.

As did Chicago's famed Auditorium Building, which was built in 1889 from the plans of Adler and Sullivan, Carnegie Hall held offices and other facilities in addition to an auditorium. The New York building, however, showed some few classical points in its design, probably more because of the location change than as a concession to the coming classicism. While the Chicago tower is undecorated, its New York counterpart is more traditional. The balustrades that top cornices and surround balconies approach classical models. But the bizarre lack of balance in the building's elevations show that classicism's general acceptance, which was to come with the Chicago World's Fair, was still two years in the future.

The building does have excellent acoustics, and was the site of most major New York musical events until it was superseded by Max Abramovitz's Philharmonic Hall at Lincoln Center. Carnegie Hall's Chicagoness makes it unusual in New York City, and, fortunately for New York's pageant of architectural history, the talk of demolition for the structure has, for the time being, ceased.

New York, New York   William Burnet Tuthill, Architect
CARNEGIE HALL

Madison Square Garden

New York, New York

McKim, Mead and White, *Architects*

Each successive Madison Square Garden has been New York City's foremost indoor arena. The first Madison Square Garden appeared when Gilmore's Concert Garden, housed in a converted railway freight station, changed name not long after its 1870 opening as an arena. The best of the Garden's several homes was the freight station's replacement, which Stanford White, of McKim, Mead and White, designed, and which opened in 1891. The structure was superseded in 1925 by a building by Tex Rickard which, unlike its predecessors, did not adjoin Madison Square. That building was in 1968 superseded in turn by the uninteresting present structure, to make way for which the great Pennsylvania Station (shown earlier in this book) was demolished.

Behind the long Twenty-sixth Street facade was a concert hall and theater to the left and a gigantic arena to the right. The most prominent feature of the beautiful building was the main tower that culminated in the Diana weathervane by Augustus St. Gaudens, which is now in the Philadelphia Museum of Art.

Of all the structures designed by Stanford White, Madison Square Garden was the architect's favorite. He kept an apartment in the building, which he preferred to occupy over his nearby Gramercy Park townhouse. Tragically, it was in Madison Square Garden that Harry Thaw in 1906 fatally shot Stanford White.

New York, New York　　　　　*McKim, Mead and White, Architects*

MADISON SQUARE GARDEN

MADISON SQUARE GARDEN—TOWER

MADISON SQUARE GARDEN—WEATHERVANE
As currently seen in the Philadelphia Museum of Art

Symphony Hall

Boston, Massachusetts

Mc Kim, Mead and White, *Architects*

Major Henry Lee Higginson, the unusual man who founded the Boston Symphony Orchestra, and for forty years ran it and paid all its debts out of his own pocket, also led the campaign to get the orchestra a permanent home. Charles Follen McKim, of McKim, Mead and White, began the plans for the hall in 1893. Wallace Clement Sabine, a Harvard physicist, was a painstaking adviser on acoustics. The $750,000 building was opened on 15 October 1900 with a concert by the Boston Symphony Orchestra, conducted by William Gericke.

A short flight of stairs leads to the front entrance, where an arrangement of eight Ionic columns supports an entablature. The long building, faced mainly with brick, consists of a high, gabled center section as wide as the entablature, and lower side section as high as the entablature.

The actual auditorium is rectangular with two balconies, and occupies most of the structure's high section, with the lower sides providing the side corridors, which, together with the front corridors, hold 22 doors to the auditorium. A series of niches around the auditorium's upper walls contain casts of 18 famous statues. The hall seats 2,631; the seats at the rear of the main floor rise on removable platforms. The stage, the floor space of which is too small, is beautifully decorated by an Aeolian-Skinner organ designed by G. Donald Harrison and installed in 1949.

Symphony Hall is not one of McKim's best buildings. The exterior bears a strong resemblance to an army structure, the Army War College built later in Washington, and shown in this book, and the design seems better suited to the military edifice. The vast, angular emptiness of Symphony Hall might have been avoided by shortening and heightening the auditorium itself, and rounding its walls. Still, McKim is probably America's greatest architect, and entitled to a miss now and then, since it is always such a near miss.

SYMPHONY HALL—AUDITORIUM

Boston, Massachusetts   *McKim, Mead and White, Architects*
SYMPHONY HALL

The New Theatre
New York, New York
Carrere and Hastings, *Architects*

The slow, northward procession of the New York City theater district halted once and for all at Times Square early in the twentieth century. Nevertheless, at Central Park West between Sixty-second and Sixty-third Streets, a location well north of Times Square, was built in 1903 the New Theater (later called the Century Theater), with which Carrere and Hastings fashioned one of the most beautiful theaters the city of theaters ever held.

Two nearly identical sides, perpendicular to each other, were joined by a jutting bay. Entrance to the theater was provided through a series of doors in the building's rusticated base. Each side, above the five doors in its base, bore five large arches, every arch having an Ionic column on either side; the bay, above its base, bore rectangular windows. Even the theater's exterior was surpassed in grandeur by its interior. The audience sat at orchestra level and on three balconies in an auditorium of rich detail.

Despite the beauty of the building, the theater did not become popular with the public, probably because of its location too far from the center of entertainment activity. The building was to become one of the city's first great classical structures to be demolished for a modern apartment house.

New York, New York   *Carrere and Hastings, Architects*

THE NEW THEATER

THE NEW THEATER—AUDITORIUM

THE NEW THEATER—CENTRAL PAVILION OF ROOF GARDEN

17
And Structures of All Sorts

Beauty is a central aim of art: to leave something beautiful where before there was nothing at all. The modernists reject the idea "beauty" out and out (except to use the word in expressing efficiency) and thereby lock themselves forever outside the realm of real art.

Beauty was a central aim of the Gilded Age architect: beauty not only in every sort of building, but also in railroad cars, boats, fire hydrants, lampposts, traffic signals. Not only should the creations of man be made beautiful, but also their arrangement, through town planning and rural planning, as well as should the arrangement of the works of nature through garden design and landscape architecture. Ideally, according to Gilded Age thought, beauty ought to be wherever there is man.

34 Gramercy Park

New York, New York

George da Cunha, *Architect*

Apartment buildings constructed for that purpose had been rare in America; there was little need for them, since even the poorest family could usually buy, rent, or themselves build a house of their own. By 1880, land had begun to be dear, especially in crowded cities, and apartment buildings then began to appear. Henry Hardenbergh's 1880–1884 building, The Dakota, (the name coming from its site's isolation at Central Park West and Seventy-second Street from the more populous areas of New York) was a trend setter for deluxe apartments, soon leading to such as 34 Gramercy Park, built in 1882–1883 from the designs of George da Cunha.

For a building in the romantic tradition, the apartment house has pronounced symmetry and decoration. Enclosed within a highly ornamental fence, the structure rises to ten stories. The first two of these are brownstone, and contain rich carving and an impressive entranceway, where a flight of steps runs between two pairs of original columns that support a lintel reading simply "Gramercy." Seven stories of brick, with many outcroppings of stringcourses that sometimes bear relief human faces, terminate in the top story, which is contained within a mansard roof. Two engaged turrets of unequal height surround a center court that divides the façade.

The apartment house faces Gramercy Park, New York City's last private park. Fortunately, the forces that want to open the park to the public have been unsuccessful; they do not realize the owners have the same right to exclude anyone from their park as from their living rooms, and that an influx of outsiders would give the park the same downtrodden look that afflicts the rest of the parks in the city's most populated areas. Samuel Ruggles, the park's founder, created a private park, and was adamant about keeping it green: "Man makes buildings but God makes space."

New York, New York   *George da Cunha, Architect*

APARTMENT HOUSE AT 34 GRAMERCY PARK

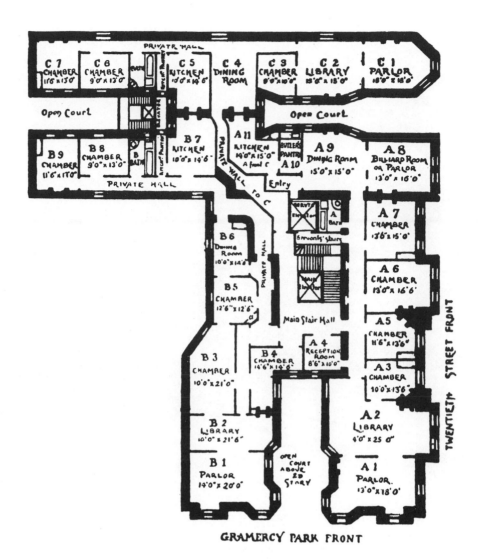

34 GRAMERCY PARK—TYPICAL FLOOR PLAN

Alexander: Private Railroad Car
of A. A. MacLeod

Pullman Company, *Builders*

Railroads being the prize industry of the Gilded Age, the prize possession of a Gilded Age millionaire was often his private railroad car. The *Alexander* was commissioned from the Pullman Company in 1890 by Angus Archibald MacLeod, president of the Philadelphia and Reading Railroad (two stations of which line appear earlier in this volume). Although the Reading was the home route

of the car, the *Alexander* was strictly a private car.

The 70-foot car was delicately decorated from its clerestory to even its pair of six-wheel trucks. The railings around the car's platforms are particularly sumptuous, and the windows and their placement unusually graceful. The interior was slightly stuffy Victorian, but nevertheless richly appointed. It must have been the interior that displeased MacLeod; two years later he ordered the Pullman Company to build a replacement—the finished product was better on the inside, and worse on the out—and he christened it also *Alexander.*

Pullman Company, Builders
ALEXANDER: PRIVATE RAILROAD CAR OF A. A. MACLEOD

ALEXANDER—SALON

ALEXANDER—END VIEW

ALEXANDER—DINING AREA

S.S. *St. Louis*

William Cramp and Sons Ship and Engine Building Company, *Builders*

An ocean crossing had always been arduous at best, but the Gilded Age, with its flair for elegant living, undertook to relieve the problem, mainly by trying to take the sea out of sea-going. This era launched the luxury liner, hotels afloat that surrounded the passengers with the same type of setting they were accustomed to ashore.

Liner development, accordingly, kept pace with architectural advances on dry land. By the closing years of the Gilded Age, liners never surpassed to this day in splendor were on the waves. These ships included the 1912 British *Titanic,* whose lasting fame was found elsewhere than in her decor, and the sublime *France,* of the same year.

Earlier in the era, when the grand Gilded Age mansion was just emerging, there also appeared the *St. Louis.* This 1895 ship did not approach in size or decoration the later ships of the period, but certainly it was an improvement over the tortuous vessels of an earlier day and pointed the way to new magnificence.

Built at the noted Cramp shipyards in Philadelphia, the 11,629-ton ship was 535 feet long and 63 feet wide. Such interiors as the library and the smoking room retained a Victorian flavor, but this was less present in the amazing dining room, with its sculpture and barrel-vault clerestory.

The *St. Louis* sailed its maiden voyage from New York to Southampton, and went on to make numerous Atlantic crossings as a commercial passenger ship. It served during the Spanish-American War as an auxiliary cruiser, and under the name *Louisville* was used by the U. S. Government during World War I. In 1920, while being refitted for civilian duty, the ship was damaged by fire. The liner was then sold to be an exhibition ship, but it was never used in that way. It was towed to Italy in 1923, where it was scrapped.

William Cramp and Sons Ship and Engine Building Company, Builders
S. S. *St. Louis*

S. S. *St. Louis*—Dining Salon

S. S. *St. Louis*—Smoking Room

S. S. *St. Louis*—Library

Interborough Rapid Transit Company Powerhouse

New York, New York

McKim, Mead and White, *Architects*

Modern architects seem to take more pleasure in giving a little gracefulness to the design of factories than of any other type structure, because the function of factories seems to fit the scientific stance that modern art likes to assume. The Gilded Age architect considered the factory like every other building in that it ought to be beautiful. Accordingly was built the Interborough Rapid Transit Company Powerhouse, which supplied electricity to the first New York City subway, which began operation in 1904. The architects for the powerhouse were McKim, Mead and White.

A plain basement of stone presents repeated sets of three long grills. Upon the basement rise brick walls, with, along the most impressive side, 17 two-story arched windows, above which runs a string-course beneath a row of triple rectangular windows and the cornice. Five smokestacks wear handsome, metal crowns.

Due to the building's purpose, the architects had no choice but to make it functional. Due to the structure's nature, a design had to be conceived that was rugged and straightforward. But these requirements were no hindrance at all to achieving the splendor which, due to the City Beautiful movement, was mandatory in the building's appearance.

New York, New York　　　　　*McKim, Mead and White, Architects*
INTERBOROUGH RAPID TRANSIT COMPANY POWERHOUSE

Manhattan Bridge

New York and Brooklyn, New York

Gustav Lindenthal, *Engineer*
Carrere and Hastings, *Architects*

The Gilded Age, which so admired technology, took great pride in constructing bridges, the era's horizontal skyscrapers. The building of the Brooklyn Bridge and its 1883 opening were followed the world over. For the Manhattan Bridge, the next bridge up the East River from the Brooklyn Bridge, was executed a design of unusual grandeur even for a Gilded Age bridge.

Gustav Lindenthal was the engineer and Carrere and Hastings the architects for the bridge that was designed in 1905 and whose construction continued into the 1920s. The span is suspended from two steel towers, and restrained at either end by a massive stone-clad abutment of exceptional beauty. The Manhattan side of the bridge boasts a monumental arch, with engaged obelisks on its piers and with wings of Tuscan colonnades that curve forward. The Brooklyn approach held allegorical statues of Manhattan and Brooklyn by Daniel Chester French; these sculptures now stand in front of the Brooklyn Museum.

New York and Brooklyn, New York

Gustav Lindenthal, Engineer
Carrere and Hastings, Architects

MANHATTAN BRIDGE

18
Epilogue

In May of 1869, the Central Pacific and the Union Pacific joined at Promontory Point, Utah, to create the transcontinental railroad; the nation was one, industry had triumphed, and there was cause for the great expectations that made the Gilded Age. In April of 1912, the *Titanic,* which an age sated with optimism had declared, in an act of hubris unsurpassed in Greek tragedy, "the ship God Himself could not sink," set out on its fated maiden voyage. Of British registry, but symbolic of the state of mind of both the U.K. and the U.S., the transatlantic liner took down with it not only people named Astor, Guggenheim, and Widener, but also the optimism that was the Gilded Age.

Classicism in American architecture began to decline soon after this symbolic disaster, and by 1915 entered a transitional stage, like the one it had been in during the 1880s and early 1890s, but in reverse. What the *Titanic* and the anticipation and realization of the First World War began, the Great Depression finished, and, by 1930, in a world made pessimistic by repeated tragedy, modernism became the dominant force in American architecture.

By World War I, the building of townhouses had come close to a halt in the most crowded cities; rising property taxes put those people who would have owned townhouses into apartments (which, however, were very spacious, especially compared with apartments being built today), or into the suburbs, since commutation by train, and, with the 1920s, by automobile, was easy. In smaller cities, though, townhouses continued to be built. Architects such as William Lawrence Bottomley produced American adaptations of traditional European styles, such as the Golsan-Cauthorne house in Richmond, Virginia. This 1917 building possesses the symmetry of its Georgian style, although the door has been placed to one side.

In the suburbs during this transitional period, classical houses were built that were generally smaller but no less elegant. Some mansions of Gilded Age size were erected, such as Whitemarsh Hall, which Horace Trumbauer designed for Edward Townsend Stotesbury. The 147-room mansion was constructed on a 400-acre estate, with appropriate gardens by Jacques Greber, at Wyndmoor, Pennsylvania, in 1916–1920. Stotesbury died in 1938, and after Mrs. Stotesbury's death in 1946, the grounds were broken up for ghastly little houses, and the mansion became the world's most beautiful chemistry laboratory. Today it is abandoned, and in pitiful condition, destroyed by local children.

Richmond, Virginia   *William Lawrence Bottomley, Architect*

RESIDENCE OF HENRY LOGAN GOLSAN

Wyndmoor, Pennsylvania   *Horace Trumbauer, Architect*

WHITEMARSH HALL: RESIDENCE OF EDWARD TOWNSEND STOTESBURY

Mr. Stotesbury was a Morgan partner, but not until his marriage in 1912 to his second wife, the former Eva Cromwell of Washington, did he begin to think hard about society. The pair bought an immense so-called cottage in Bar Harbor, and deciding it was unsuitable, had it torn down, and another built in its place. Upon first inspection, they found the new cottage also to be unsuitable, had it torn down, and another built in its place.

Their greatest social triumphs came in Florida, where Mrs. Stotesbury became known as "The Queen of Palm Beach Society." El Mirasol, their home in that city, was a successful American version of Mediterranean architecture, which similarly spawned the Hollywood, California, style. The

architect for the Stotesbury setting was Addison Mizner, who had been a miner and prizefighter, and was now a self-taught architect.

Palm Beach's gigantic Royal Poinciana Hotel departed this earth in 1934, after much hurricane damage, but is survived to this day by another Flagler hotel, the Breakers. The present structure, which has now been enlarged to 600 rooms, was built in 1925 as successor to two previous buildings, the first, which originally was called the Palm Beach Lodge, having been built in 1895, and the second in 1906. The architects for the current Breakers were Schultze and Weaver, who designed New York City's present Waldorf-Astoria. The style of the hotel is Mediterranean, which is in fact classical.

Palm Beach, Florida *Addison Mizner, Architect*
EL MIRASOL: WINTER RESIDENCE OF EDWARD TOWNSEND STOTESBURY

Palm Beach, Florida　　　　　　　　　*Schultze and Weaver, Architects*

THE BREAKERS

The most sumptuous of many grand interiors is the circular dining room, which is divided by a wonderful screen and topped by a magnificent ceiling with skylight.

The traditional styles and their decorative beauty were still acceptable for more personal buildings, such as homes and hotels, but for more commercial structures these styles were in trouble. In the famous design competition during the early 1920s for the Chicago Tribune Building, the more beautiful Gothic plan by Hood and Howells won out, but much sympathy was had for the runner-up, a stripped-down (for then), modern (for then) design by Eliel Saarinen, and the consensus of opinion when the

controversy was settled was that skyscrapers should be modern. The better building won the competition, but the better styles lost in the long run.

In the forward march to modernism, retrogression to romanticism was clear. The Bowery Savings Bank, which at the end of the last century had commissioned McKim, Mead and White to design that splendid classical temple that still stands on the street from which the bank took its name, now commissioned the design for a new headquarters from York and Sawyer, the architects of such noble classical banks as the main office of the Brooklyn Trust Company. (Both earlier banks are shown earlier in this book.) After years of almost complete absence,

Chicago, Illinois   *Hood and Howells, Architects*

CHICAGO TRIBUNE TOWER

Eliel Saarinen, Architect

CHICAGO TRIBUNE TOWER—PROJECT
Runner-up design.

New York, New York   *York and Sawyer, Architects*
BOWERY SAVINGS BANK, FORTY-SECOND STREET

BOWERY SAVINGS BANK, FORTY-SECOND STREET—MAIN BANKING ROOM

the style of the Bowery headquarters, which opened in 1923, was—of all things—Romanesque.

But this was Romanesque of quality never bettered in American architecture. The grandeur of the vast arch that leads to the main banking room at street level in the 18-story building, and that room's rich interior decoration, which includes the marble floor reminiscent of that of the Brooklyn Trust, the column shafts, each of one of six different types of marble, the fine sculpture of capitals, corbels, and cages: all suggest this Romanesque has been greatly influenced and improved by the architectural developments during the near disappearance of that romantic style.

By 1930, as has been said, modernism held the upper hand, even for many private homes. Still, perfect classical buildings continued to be erected. Among these are San Francisco's War Memorial Opera House and War Memorial Veterans Building, both designed by Arthur Brown, Jr., in 1932 as companions for his earlier City Hall. While these structures show not a trace of modernism, other classical buildings had been influenced by the new movement. This explains the plain wings of Washington's Supreme Court Building, constructed in 1935 from the designs of Cass Gilbert. In the same city, the exterior of the National Gallery, designed in 1938 by John Russell Pope, while still totally classical, clearly showed the effects of modernism.

World War II ended the ebullient optimism the Gilded Age had known and brought the triumph of modernism.

The Gilded Age is the best era of American architecture, but why must this be so? Why does the present restrain itself from surpassing the architecture of the past? Why does man hold himself back from building in the great styles of the past, which would become the great styles of the future? Everywhere casual observers of architecture are heard to remark, "That's a nice building. It must be old."

Today's architecture is bad because the present has taken modern architecture as the only possible

San Francisco, California   *Arthur Brown, Jr., Architect*
WAR MEMORIAL OPERA HOUSE

style and because modern architecture is a dismal failure. It is a success numerically: it has been predominant since the 1930s, making inapplicable the apology that every new art movement is shunned in the beginning. Artistically, however, it is a flop; it is unloved by public and even by patron and—*mirabile dictu*—often by architect. It would seem buildings in this style would cease to be built, particularly in America, a nation with a tendency to reject any idea that does not work.

In fact, modern architecture as represented in the works of Wright, Le Corbusier, and the like has died out. It has, however, bequeathed the world a descendant even more hateful than itself; the tenets of modern architecture have been taken to such extremes as to create a new style which might be called the "no-style." The no-style is the ultimate product of "form follows function": simply a utilitarian building with no pretense at art, and without even the personality—however bland or otherwise unfortunate it might have been—of the previously modern modern architecture.

The new derivative can now be seen throughout America, even in New York City, where until recently patrons tried to show some sort of impressive facade to the world. The clearest example of the no-style is to be found in the suburban apartment house near every city. How fitting that this style, which is an absence of architecture, should bloom first in buildings of this use, the sudden rash of suburban apartment buildings being a symbol of the declining American standard of living. These structures are generally of brick (common bond throughout); brick is used not for any aesthetic reason, but because brick can be reasonably cheap and needs little maintenance. Undecorated walls—outside and in—and windows and doors haphazardly placed might be sanctioned by modernism, but are really that way because no reason can be seen to do otherwise, and modern theory lets the builder get away with it. An occasional mansard roof might be construed as a classical touch, but it is present because it is cheaper than using brickwork all the way to the roof level. Surprisingly, the economy of a no-style structure is usually slight over that of a classical structure (which, also surprisingly, is generally less expensive than a traditionally modern one), but design quality is of no consequence, so any saving is worthwhile. The no-style building makes no attempt at beauty, or even at the modern virtue of shock: it is just a shelter.

Apparently architecture no longer has any need of the architect. Throughout the ages, building design's technical aspects—which for most buildings are not very difficult—have usually been handled as a matter of course by the architect, his main job being to see to the building's aesthetics. With the coming of the skyscraper came the consulting engineer, who saw to the technical design, while the architect continued to care for the building's appearance. With the flowering of modernism, form did follow function, until today the architect strives to give the building the scientific look that naturally derives from the engineer's work. What is needed to make the architect obsolete once and for all is the engineer who is trained slightly in aesthetics. Certainly such a person could look after the minor matter of the building's appearance, while still performing his major role of supervising the building's technical design.

With such a step as the emergence of this engineer, the art of architecture becomes merely an enhancing touch, like the art of movie set decorating or the art of television commercial writing. For such art there will always be a market, but for art as it is generally thought of—drama, sculpture, painting, poetry—the future may have no need. Man seems about to enter a world without art.

Just as people now speak of the Iron Age, so they may in the future refer to the Art Age. As is more and more the case today, art of the past may become exclusively the realm of scholars, who study it for its history and its historical value.

Man appears to have outlived his need for art. It told of sufferings and exaltations that he shies away from in the new shockproof world of human equivalence he has secured for himself. But as most sculpture loses its significance without architecture to define its place, so every man loses his bearings without art. When every man gains his own equal share of this whole value-free, feeling-free new world, what becomes of his soul, that thing the psychologists rush to assure him he has not got?

Brief Lives of Some Well-Known Gilded Age Architects

Daniel H. Burnham

Born in Henderson, New York, Daniel Hudson Burnham (1846–1912) moved at eight years old with his family to Chicago, where he lived the rest of his life and where his architectural practice was always based. His apprenticeship was under William LeBaron Jenney, a leading architect of that city. In 1873, Burnham joined with John Wellborn Root (1850–1892) to create Burnham and Root. Following the death of Root, Burnham worked independently, then in 1896, took on partners to form D. H. Burnham and Company.

Like other Chicago architects of his time, Burnham was intrigued by the new construction techniques then becoming available, and he wed them to classical designs.

Burnham was chief architect for the World's Columbian Exposition held at Chicago in 1893, an event of great importance in the development of American classical architecture. His knowledge of classicism and of City Beautiful planning led him to play a large part in the designing of the cities of Washington, Cleveland, Detroit, Manila, San Francisco, and Chicago itself.

He died on a visit to Heidelberg, Germany, leaving two sons, D. H., Jr., and Hubert, both architects.

Carrere and Hastings

One of the foremost architectural firms based in New York City, Carrere and Hastings designs were predominantly classical.

John Merwin Carrere (1858–1911) was born in Rio de Janeiro, Brazil, the son of a coffee merchant from Baltimore. The young man was educated in Europe, especially at the École des Beaux Arts. He received his diploma from that school in 1882, and entered the New York office of McKim, Mead and White in the following year.

Thomas Hastings (1860–1929), born in New York, was the son of Dr. Thomas S. Hastings, a Presbyterian minister. The son was schooled at Columbia and the École des Beaux Arts.

The two architects formed their partnership in 1884, and soon attracted their best customer, Henry M. Flagler, who over the years ordered many buildings for Florida, which he played a large part in developing.

Carrere lived during his years of practice first in Staten Island, then in Manhattan; Hastings in New York, with a country house in Westbury, Long Island. Carrere's death resulted from an auto accident of two weeks earlier. Hastings died after an operation for appendicitis.

Cass Gilbert

Born at Zanesville, Ohio, Cass Gilbert (1858–1934) was raised at St. Paul, Minnesota. His apprenticeship at a St. Paul architectural office was followed by study at M.I.T. He went to Europe for part of 1880, and later in that same year entered the office of McKim, Mead and White. He returned to St. Paul in 1882, where he worked with James Knox Taylor (1857–1929) as Gilbert and Taylor. Ten years later the partnership was dissolved. For St. Paul, Gilbert designed the Minnesota State Capitol, built 1896–1903; he later was the architect for the state capitols of Arkansas and West Virginia. During most of his career his office was in New York City. He resided during his later years in Ridgefield, Connecticut, where he died. His son, Cass Gilbert, Jr., was also an architect.

Richard Morris Hunt

Richard Morris Hunt (1827–1895) was born in Brattleboro, Vermont. In adolescence, he was taken to live in Europe by his mother. He attended the École des Beaux Arts, then traveled in Europe and Egypt. In 1854, he entered the office of Victor Lafuel, and worked on the Louvre and the Tuilleries.

Hunt returned to the United States in 1855, when he opened his own office, which he ran as an atelier. His early work was romantic, but he soon realized these styles were insufficient for the new age, and so he became the architect who led America back to classicism and who created Gilded Age architecture on its grand scale.

As the ranking Gilded Age architect at the time of the 1893 World's Columbian Exposition in Chicago, Hunt designed the Administration Building, the central and tallest edifice of the fair. He holds the structure in his hands in the Central Park monument to him, which faces the Frick Collection.

McKim, Mead and White

McKim, Mead and White is generally considered to have been the leading architectural firm in the U.S. during the Gilded Age. Their first buildings were romantic, but the partners showed an early interest in classicism, and built trend-setting structures in that style. Their office was located in New York City.

Charles Follen McKim (1847–1909), probably the most talented of the three, was born in Chester County, Pennsylvania, and received his early schooling in the public schools of Philadelphia. At 19, he entered Lawrence Scientific School at Cambridge, Massachusetts, to become a mining engineer. He soon turned to architecture, and was apprenticed to Russell Sturgis, later attending the École des Beaux Arts, then traveling widely in Europe. When he returned to America, his family had moved to Orange, New Jersey, outside New York. He entered the office of Gambrill and Richardson there, at eight dollars per week as a draftsman.

In 1872, he went into partnership with William Mead; the pair were joined in 1878 by William Bigelow, to form McKim, Mead and Bigelow. The new member withdrew in the following year, and was replaced by Stanford White.

McKim became much honored, receiving honorary degrees from Columbia, Harvard, and Princeton. With Daniel H. Burnham and Frederick Law Olmsted, Jr., he was a principal in the replanning of Washington. McKim was a principal founder of the American Academy in Rome. He lived for many years at 13 East Thirty-fifth Street, New York, but in January 1908, moved to St. James, Long Island, where he spent his last days.

William Rutherford Mead (1846–1928) was born and raised in Brattleboro, Massachusetts, and graduated from Amherst. He joined the firm of Russell Sturgis, then traveled abroad before becoming the partner of McKim in 1872.

Mead retired as head of the firm in 1920, and was replaced by William Mitchell Kendall. The elder architect then went abroad to live, and is buried in Florence, beside his brother, Larkin G. Mead, the sculptor.

Stanford White (1853–1906) was born in New York, the son of Richard Grant White, the Shakespearean scholar. At 18, Stanford White graduated from New York University, and at 19, entered Gambrill and Richardson as a draftsman. He met McKim in France and traveled with him, the partnership resulting.

Harry Thaw shot Stanford White in the head, killing him instantly, over the affections of a woman. The murder took place at the summer opening of the Garden Roof Show at Madison Square Garden, which White had designed. He left a son, also an architect, Lawrence Grant White.

Peabody and Stearns

Boston's leading architectural firm during the Gilded Age, the primary work of Peabody and Stearns was classical, which they used in the reserved and dignified buildings desired by that city.

Robert Swain Peabody (1845–1917) was born in New Bedford, Massachusetts, son of Rev. Ephraim Peabody, minister of King's Chapel in Boston. After graduation from Harvard in 1866, he studied in Europe, particularly at the École des Beaux Arts. Returning to Boston in 1870, he formed the partnership with Stearns.

John Goddard Stearns (1843–1917) was born in New York City, but was raised in Brookline, Massachusetts, where he continued to reside throughout his life. He graduated from Lawrence Scientific School at Cambridge, Massachusetts, in 1863, after which he entered the Boston office of Ware and Van Brunt, before joining Peabody in 1870.

The partners had a close working relationship, and Peabody died less than three weeks after Stearns.

John Russell Pope

Born in New York City, John Russell Pope (1874–1937) was the son of artist John Pope. The young man went to the College of the City of New York and studied architecture under William R. Ware at Columbia's School of Mines. In 1895, he won the McKim Rome Scholarship, and in 1896, the Schermerhorn Scholarship, both enabling him to spend time in Europe. From Rome, he went to the École des Beaux Arts at Paris, where he was awarded a diploma in 1900. He worked for a brief time in the office of Bruce Price. Pope then opened his own office in New York.

Generally, his buildings are strictly classical. Pope's structures in Washington are best known, but his buildings were erected around the world, including the Duveen wing of the British Museum, the new sculpture hall of the Tate Gallery, and the U.S. Government Building, all in London, and the American Battle Monument at Montfaucon, France.

Pope died in New York, after becoming sick at The Waves, the Newport residence built in 1927 and still standing, which he designed for himself.

George B. Post

George Brown Post (1837–1913) received military schooling in his native Ossining, New York, and studied civil engineering at New York University before entering Hunt's atelier. In 1860, Post went into partnership with Charles D. Gambrill (1832–1880), but they closed their offices at the onset of the Civil War, in which Post rose to the rank of colonel. He returned to architectural practice in 1867.

Post was especially interested in the planning and structure of buildings. For example, he is responsible for the present-day hotel plan of a bath to every room, as in his Statler Hotel, built in Buffalo in 1911–1912.

He died at his country house in Bernardsville, New Jersey.

Bruce Price

Bruce Price (1843–1903) was born and raised in Cumberland, Maryland. In 1862, he entered the Baltimore office of Niernsee and Nelson, architects. After a year in Paris, he returned to Baltimore where he went into partnership with Ephraim Baldwin (1837–1916). After Price's marriage in 1873, he opened an office in his wife's hometown of Wilkes-Barre, Pennsylvania, but from 1877 on his office was in New York City. He died in Paris, en route to Tokyo where was to be built to his plans a palace for the Crown Prince of Japan. His daughter was Emily Price Post, the etiquette authority; her son, Bruce Price Post, was an architect.

Horace Trumbauer

The son of a traveling salesman, Horace Trumbauer (1868–1938) was born in Bucks County, Pennsylvania. At 16, the young man became a draftsman for the Philadelphia firm of G. W. Hewitt (1841–1916) and W. D. Hewitt (1848–1924). At 21, he went on his own as an architect. When 24, he received the commission for the immense country mansion of William Welsh Harrison, Gray Towers (now Beaver College) in Glenside, Pennsylvania. Many fine commissions followed, in and out of the Philadelphia area.

Trumbauer, whose office was always in Philadelphia, was at home in all styles, but particularly favored that of eighteenth-century France. His reputation is regaining its high position, following decades of criticism for his classicism and for his modeling his structures on other buildings, of the continuance of disparagement spread by jealous New York architects, and the lack of attention drawn by the life of a man almost totally devoted to his work.

Warren and Wetmore

One of the most creative of Gilded Age architectural firms, the New York City office of Warren and Wetmore could always be expected to do clever and beautiful things using the elements of classicism.

Charles D. Wetmore (1867–1941) was born in Elmira, New York, and graduated from Harvard in 1889.

Whitney Warren (1864–1943) was born and raised in New York. At 18, he began at the École des Beaux Arts, growing greatly enamoured with France, where he continued to live for over 10 years. He began his partnership with Wetmore in 1896.

Of all their buildings, Warren's favorite was the Louvain Library in Belgium, the earlier structure having been destroyed in World War I. Warren caused an international stir by insisting the new library bear the inscription: *Furore Teutonica Diruta—Dono Americano Restituta* (Destroyed by German Fury—Restored by American Generosity).

Warren was a co-founder of the Beaux Arts institution of Design, whose famed annual balls he presided over until their suspension in 1937. Warren had retired from architectural practice in 1931.

Glossary

ABUTMENT—solid masonry to counteract lateral thrust of a vault, a bridge, or so on

ACANTHUS—Mediterranean herbs whose leaves are adapted as decoration; used particularly in Corinthian or composite capitals

ACROTERION—a free-standing ornament placed at the apex and ends of a pediment

ANTEFIX (pl. ANTEFIXAE)—the upright ornament along the eaves of a roof

APSE—a vaulted, interior recess especially at the end of a church chancel

ARCADE—a row of arches carrying one side of a roof

ATLAS (sometimes called TELAMON)—a column in the shape of a male human

ATTIC—a wall or story above the cornice

AXIS—the imaginary center line about which a symmetrical design is set

BALUSTRADE—a railing supported by dwarf columns called balusters

BASEMENT (sometimes called GROUND LEVEL)—the level beneath the first story, even though the basement fully or partly emerges from the ground

BAY—a vertical division of a wall; also (sometimes called a BOW) an alcove that protrudes outside a building

BAY WINDOW—a bow with its own window

BRACKET—a support projecting from a wall to bear a weight

BUTTRESS—an exterior prop built fully or partly attached to a wall to which it gives support; a free-standing buttress is connected to the main body of the building by a flying buttress

CABRIOLE—in furniture, a leg curving outward near the top and inward near the bottom, where it ends in a simulated animal paw

CAPITAL—the uppermost major division of a column

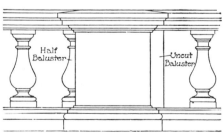

Balustrade and Balusters

Capital (Ionic)

CARYATID—a column in the shape of a female human

CHANCEL—the church section containing the altar and usually reserved for the clergy and singers

CHICAGO WINDOW—a window divided into a large, immovable sash between two smaller, movable ones

CHOIR—the church section reserved for the singers

CLERESTORY—a light-admitting story raised above the surrounding roof; also, a similar, smaller construction for admitting light or air to a railroad car

COFFER—a recessed decorative panel, usually square or rectangular

COLONNADE—a row of columns carrying one side of a roof

COLUMN—a tall, narrow support basically divided into the base (if present), the shaft, and the capital

COMPOSITE—a classical order, identified by its capital, which combines the acanthus leaves of a Corinthian capital with the scroll of an Ionic capital

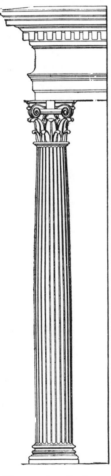

Composite Order

CORBEL—a bracket that supports a horizontal feature or upperweight, such as a beam

CORINTHIAN—a classical order, identified by the acanthus leaves, without scroll, of its capital

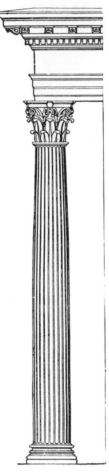

Corinthian Order

CORNICE—the projecting feature around the top of a building's walls

CRESTING—a decorative element crowning a building, or crowning such a building feature as a fireplace

CROSSING—the section of a cruciform church where nave and transept intersect

CRUCIFORM—shaped like a cross

CUPOLA—a small, free-standing enclosure on roof or dome

DADO—in interior decoration, the lower part of a wall when finished different than the part above

DENTIL—one of a row of cubes that runs across a cornice

DORIC—a Classical order, whose capitals are decorated with moulding only and whose shafts are fluted. Greek Doric columns have a squared capital and no base, while Roman Doric columns have a round base and capital

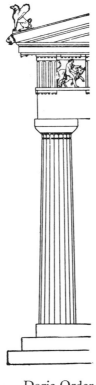

Doric Order

DORMER—a small section, bearing a window and projecting from a slanting roof

ELEVATION—one entire side of a building

ELL—a wing attached at a right angle to one end of a building section

ENGAGED—partly enveloped by an adjoining feature

ENTABLATURE—the classical feature directly supported by the columns and usually consisting of, from bottom to top, architrave, frieze, and cornice

FACADE—the main elevation of a building

FENESTRATION—the design and arrangement of windows and other openings

FESTOON (sometimes called SWAG)—a decoration resembling a chain of flowers, leaves, or ribbons

FINIAL—a small, terminal ornament atop a gable, dome, or the like

Entablature

FLUTE—one of the many vertical grooves in a column shaft. The ridge between two flutes is an arris

GABLE—an end of the type roof that slopes from a central line; also, that type roof

GIBBS SURROUND—a door or window frame of quoin-like blocks or of intermittent blocks often connected by a band

HALF-TIMBER—a construction in which the wall space between the timber frame is filled in with brick, stucco, or the like

IONIC—a classical order, identified by the scroll, without acanthus leaves, of its capital

LANTERN—a small, light-admitting structure atop a building

LIGHT—a window; also one windowpane

LINTEL—a straight, horizontal member to support weight above an opening

LOGGIA—an enclosed area open to the air at one or more sides

MANSARD—a roof of two sections, both of which slope outward on all four sides, the lower section being the steeper and higher

MEZZANINE—a low story, or apparent story, between the two main floors of a building

NAVE—the long, center section of a church, between entrance and chancel, and used mainly by the congregation

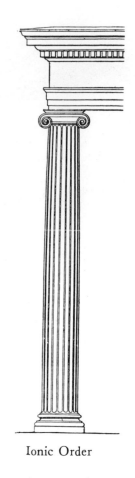

Ionic Order

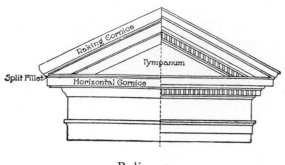

Pediment

tween the rest of the building and coach (or automobile)

PORTICO—a roof borne on columns and attached to a building

QUOIN—a prominent stone at the corner of a building

RUSTICATION—the wall of a building cut to show blocks with deep joints

SHAFT—the part of a column or pier between base and capital

SITE—the place in which a building is erected, especially as to its surroundings

SPANDREL—the wall part next to the curve of the arch

SPIRE—a sharply-pointed pyramidal roof or roof-like element

STORY (sometimes called FLOOR)—a major level outside and inside a building, regulated by the vertical position of interior rooms. The first story is the building's lowest story considered major; it is not necessarily at ground level

STRINGCOURSE—a horizontal band that divides a wall

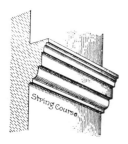

OBELISK—a four-sided pillar of stone, tapering upward, with a pyramidal top

ORDER—one of the five types of combinations of entablatures and columns in classical architecture. The five orders are named Doric, Ionic, Corinthian, Tuscan, and composite

PARAPET—a low safety wall at the side of a roof, bridge, or the like

PARTY WALL—a wall used as part of adjoining buildings

PAVILION—a major section of a building, set off in shape and placement from the main section of the building to which it is attached; also, a type of outbuilding, usually used for festive occasion

PEDIMENT—a gable above an entablature; also, a gable-like element above a door or window

PIAZZA—an open porch, a veranda

PIER—a tall, square support, acting as does a column and separated into the same orders

PILASTER—an engaged pier

PORCH—a veranda; also, a portico

PORTE-COCHERE—a shelter for people moving be-

STUCCO—an exterior finish of cement, sand, and lime

SWAG—a festoon

TERRA-COTTA—a type of hard, fired clay

TRACERY—a delicate arrangement of ribs, bars, or the like, as in a Gothic building

TRANSEPT—a church section that crosses the nave; also, the main section that does so

TURRET—a small tower, usually engaged in a larger structure

TUSCAN—a classical order, identified by the absence of fluting in its shaft

VAULT—a curved roof, using the principle of the arch. A barrel vault resembles half a cylinder.

VERMICULATION—the carving of surfaces to resemble worm tracks

VITRUVIAN SCROLL (sometimes called RUNNING DOG)—a carving found in bands and resembling an ocean wave

WIDOW'S WALK—a platform on the roof of a building, especially in New England

WING—a building section that projects from a center structure

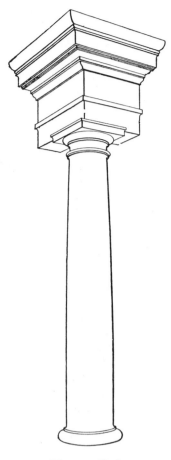

Tuscan Order

Suggestions for Further Reading

The Penguin Dictionary of Architecture, by John Fleming, Hugh Honour, and Nikolaus Pevsner (2nd ed. Baltimore: Penguin Books, 1972) gives help with the basic problem of architectural terms.

The lives of many Gilded Age architects are contained in another useful reference work, *Biographical Dictionary of American Architects (Deceased)* by Henry F. Withey and Elsie Rathburn Withey (Los Angeles: New Age Publishing Company, 1956; reissued Los Angeles: Hennessey and Ingalls).

The publication of buildings by Gilded Age traditional architects has been spotty, although each major architect deserves a catalogue similar to *A Monograph of the Work of McKim, Mead and White* (New York: Architectural Book Publishing Company, 1917, four volumes). A number of architects of that era were treated in their own day by long, illustrated articles in architectural magazines. The Gilded Age architects that laid the way for the modern are well published today, and so are developments that anticipated modernism, as did *The Shingle Style and the Stick Style* by Vincent J. Scully, Jr. (rev. ed. New Haven: Yale University Press, 1971).

Some Gilded Age traditional buildings can be found in architectural guidebooks to individual cities, and some types of structures have books devoted to them, as do country estates in *American Estates and Gardens* by Barr Ferree (New York: Munn and Company, 1906).

The best introduction to Gilded Age interiors is *The Decoration of Houses* by Edith Wharton and Ogden Codman, Jr. (2nd ed. New York: Charles Scribner's Sons, 1907), the first book by the famous American authoress, who wrote it in collaboration with one of the nation's finest architects. The book can be used also for guidance in present-day decorating, since such good design may have gone out of fashion but cannot go out of style.

The idea of reviving traditional modes for use today is vigorously desired in *The Golden City* by Henry Hope Reed (rev. ed. New York: W. W. Norton and Company, 1971), which sets forth clearly the controversy between traditional and modern. The need in architecture for beauty and the ability of traditional styles to provide it easily is shown in *The City of Man* by Christopher Tunnard (rev. ed. New York: Charles Scribner's Sons, 1971), and the importance of traditional styles, especially the classical, to human beings is inspiringly proved in *The Architecture of Humanism* by Geoffrey Scott (paperback ed. New York: Charles Scribner's Sons, 1969).

A good deal of information on Gilded Age classical structures can be found in the publications of an organization now fostering the revival of classicism: Classical America, New York City.

Photographic Credits

Photos courtesy Allegheny County Commissioners: 209-10

Wayne Andrews: 40, 92

Courtesy, Biltmore House and Gardens, Asheville, N. C.: 59-62

Boston Public Library: 232-34

Fletcher W. Brodie: 186

H. Stafford Bryant, Jr.: 271 top

Cathedral Church of St. John the Divine: 195-96

Cathedral Church of St. Peter and St. Paul: 202 (Bernie Boston, Washington *Evening Star News*), 203-4

Columbia University Libraries: 236

Photo by Con Edison: 262

Collection of Raymond D. Entine: 79 top

Henry Morrison Flagler Museum: 118-20, 129-30, 136-37, 273

State Photographic Archives, Strozier Library, Florida State University: 272

Robert P. Foley: 109

Picture Collection, Free Library of Philadelphia: 26, 165-65, 167

Copyright The Frick Collection, New York: 48-49

Isabella Stewart Gardner Museum: 43-44

John Hopf: 99

Library of Congress: 33-36, 41-42, 230-31

The Mariners Museum: 266-67

Museum Division, Metro Dade County Park & Recreation Department: 124-26

Metropolitan Museum of Art, Photography by Robert Gray: 249

Minneapolis Institute of Arts: 253

M. I. T. Photos: 225-26

Pierpont Morgan Library, Ezra Stoller © Esto: 239-40

Museum of Fine Arts, Boston: 251-52

Museum of the City of New York: 18, 22, 24-25, 30, 140, 162 (Berenice Abbott for Federal Art Project "Changing New York"), 178, 184, 214, 269

National Gallery of Art: 277

National Lawn Tennis Hall of Fame and Tennis Museum: 145, 169 bottom

Edison National Historic Site, National Park Service, U. S. Department of the Interior: 10 top, 53-55

Vanderbilt National Historic Site, National Park Service, U. S. Department of the Interior: 64-66

Newport Historical Society: 169 center left and right

Public Information Office, The New York Public Library: 241 (Parker), 242 (O. E. Nelson), 243

Historical Society of Pennsylvania: 81 bottom, 271 bottom

Office of the City Representative, City of Philadelphia: 15 bottom

Philadelphia Museum of Art: 121-23 (copied by A. J. Wyatt, Staff Photographer), 257 bottom

Index

A number in *italics* indicates that an illustration of the topic is found on that page.